Christoph Martin Wieland as the Originator of
Modern Travesty in German Literature

UNC | COLLEGE OF ARTS AND SCIENCES
Germanic and Slavic Languages and Literatures

From 1949 to 2004, UNC Press and the UNC Department of Germanic & Slavic Languages and Literatures published the UNC Studies in the Germanic Languages and Literatures series. Monographs, anthologies, and critical editions in the series covered an array of topics including medieval and modern literature, theater, linguistics, philology, onomastics, and the history of ideas. Through the generous support of the National Endowment for the Humanities and the Andrew W. Mellon Foundation, books in the series have been reissued in new paperback and open access digital editions. For a complete list of books visit www.uncpress.org.

Christoph Martin Wieland as the Originator of Modern Travesty in German Literature

CHARLOTTE CRAIG

UNC Studies in the Germanic Languages and Literatures
Number 64

Copyright © 1970

This work is licensed under a Creative Commons CC BY-NC-ND license. To view a copy of the license, visit http://creativecommons.org/licenses.

Suggested citation: Craig, Charlotte. *Christoph Martin Wieland as the Originator of Modern Travesty in German Literature*. Chapel Hill: University of North Carolina Press, 1970. DOI: https://doi.org/10.5149/9781469657301_Craig

Library of Congress Cataloging-in-Publication Data
Names: Craig, Charlotte.
Title: Christoph Martin Wieland as the originator of modern travesty in German literature / by Charlotte Craig.
Other titles: University of North Carolina Studies in the Germanic Languages and Literatures ; no. 64.
Description: Chapel Hill : University of North Carolina Press, [1970] Series: University of North Carolina Studies in the Germanic Languages and Literatures. | Includes bibliographical references.
Identifiers: LCCN 70635052 | ISBN 978-1-4696-5729-5 (pbk: alk. paper) | ISBN 978-1-4696-5730-1 (ebook)
Subjects: Wieland, Christoph Martin, 1733-1813. | Parody.
Classification: LCC PT2571 .C68 | DCC 838/ .609

Chapter IV includes a slightly modified version of "From Folk Legend to Travesty: An Example of Wieland's Artistic Adaptations" originally published in *The German Quarterly*, Vol. 41, No. 3.

Laetus in praesens animus quod ultra est
oderit curare et amara lento
temperet risu: nihil est ab omni
    parte beatum.
                                    HORACE

PREFACE

I should like to express my sincere thanks to the University of Kansas, where this study originated under the auspices of an Elizabeth M. Watkins Faculty Fellowship.

I am grateful to Professor Kenneth Negus of Rutgers University for his encouragement and valuable counsel. To Professor John H. Fitzell of Rutgers University I extend my thanks for his interest and helpful suggestions. I also wish to express my appreciation to the editors of *The German Quarterly* for permitting me to include in Chapter IV, with slight modifications, an article of mine that had originally appeared in their journal.

My work was greatly facilitated by the courteous, efficient cooperation of The Library of Congress, the George Washington University Library, and The Milton Eisenhower Library (The Johns Hopkins University).

I gratefully acknowledge my husband's solicitude in sustaining my effort. To all who assisted me in many ways— my warm thanks.

CHARLOTTE CRAIG

CONTENTS

INTRODUCTION   1

PART I. THE THEORY

 Chapter I: THE STATE OF THE TRAVESTY IN GERMAN
    LITERATURE BEFORE WIELAND 11
 Chapter II: WIELAND'S APPROACH TO THE TRAVESTY:
    HIS SATIRICAL PENCHANT 20

PART II. WIELAND'S TRAVESTIES AND THEIR SOURCES

 Chapter III: THE NOVELS AND EPICS 33
 Chapter IV: THE LESSER GENRES 63
   1. THE SHORT MIXED NARRATIVE 63
   2. THE FAIRY TALE 87
   3. THE LEGEND 107
   4. THE FABLE 117

CONCLUSION 121

NOTES 128

BIBLIOGRAPHY 132

INDEX 140

INTRODUCTION

Christoph Martin Wieland, regarded as a prominent exponent of German Rococo literature, gained stature primarily for his novels and verse narratives. While these and many other phases of Wieland's life and work have been the subject of scholarly inquiry previously, his creative impact on the travesty in literature has received inadequate attention so far. This study seeks to augment Wieland scholarship in this heretofore unexplored area.

In 1949 Sengle summed up the status of Wieland research in these words: "Während die Erforschung...[Anderer]... liebevoll betrieben wurde und in runden, gewichtigen Monographien zusammenfassenden Ausdruck fand, macht die bisherige Wieland-Forschung den Eindruck eines Trümmerfeldes."[1] Even now, current bibliographies reveal the conspicuous lack of a unified investigation of Wieland's travesties. Likewise, no well-rounded evaluation of the travesty as a literary genre exists. The awareness that in a study linking Wieland with the travesty in German literature I would be contributing to two areas of literary inquiry has prompted the present undertaking. In addition, there is evidence of a renewed Wieland renaissance as manifested by recent editions of his works, for example, *Christoph Martin Wieland. Werke*, ed. Fritz Martini and Hans Werner Seiffert. 5 vols. (München, 1964-1968) and *Christoph Martin Wieland. Ausgewählte Werke in drei Bänden*, ed. Friedrich Beißner (München, 1964).

To establish the extent to which Wieland contributed to the area of the travesty, to investigate the poet's approach to his

1

sources, the nature and quality of his innovations, and to appraise the level and distribution of his travesties in relationship to the sum total of his literary work in general is the object of this monograph. It aims less at scrupulous completeness than at a balanced presentation of Wieland's contribution to the travesty by including mainly works of major literary interest and value.

This study is arranged in two divisions: Part I includes a chronological treatment of the state of the travesty in German literature before Wieland, and an illustration of the poet's parodistic inclination. Part II investigates Wieland's adaptations as compared with his sources. In order to achieve maximum cogency, Wieland's travesties will be considered according to types of sources from which he wrought his adaptations. Analyses of his adaptations will be presented under broad headings of specific major and lesser genres, respectively. Discussion of sources such as the novel, and the epic, will be included among the former, while the latter will contain representative sources from less demanding literary genres, *i.e.*, short mixed narrative, fairy tale, legend, and fable. This method is defensible in view of Wieland's versatility in the choice of his models; besides, it should afford insight into the matter of distribution, or the poet's preference of source material. Wieland's travesties will be arranged chronologically in each category so as to reflect changes which might be occasioned by the process of maturation and eventual decline.

Any comprehensive Wieland study is likely to present a challenge stemming from such considerations as the poet's long life and resulting influences from various philosophical or literary movements, his personal metamorphoses, his versatility, and last, but not least, his dependence upon models. Wieland was aware of his lack of originality in creating plots or conceiving characters. He admitted his shortcoming frankly, "Ich habe gar wenig Erfindungskraft," and he made a practice of acknowledging his sources.[2] In view of his contribution to the evolution of the modern travesty his apology seems to be unwarranted. Friedrich Beißner in his lecture

"Poesie des Stils" attests to the value and quality of Wieland's *Einkleidungskunst:* "Der Stoff, der aus Quellen zu schöpfende 'Grundstoff,' ist ihm etwas, das man 'finden,' das jeder 'finden' kann, für das er auch nichts zu 'erfinden' braucht; denn die dichterische Gabe der 'Erfindung' wendet er an Höheres und Wesentlicheres: er nennt es schlicht 'die *Bearbeitung* des Stoffs'—die gilt ihm allein als 'die wahre Erfindung.' Das ist seine 'Poesie des Stils.'"[3] *Einkleidung* neccessarily involves the adaptation of a model; travesty which, by definition, relies on an existing source, is the process or result of *Einkleidung* for slighting or comic effect.[4] The nature and degree of mutation of the object to be scorned, ridiculed, or otherwise to be taken to task is conditioned by its creator's disposition and level of sophistication.

In his work *Die deutsche Dichtung der Aufklärungszeit*, Ferdinand Josef Schneider cites Wieland's literary revival of the spirit of Lucianus Samosatensis as the major factor in the former's success with the travesty; at the same time, Schneider's comment serves to substantiate my inquiry and its perhaps somewhat problematic title: "Durch dieses von französischem Geist inspirierte Zurückgreifen auf Lukian wird Wieland der eigentliche Schöpfer der modernen Travestie in unserer Literatur. Er löst deutschen Dichtern die Zunge und gibt ihnen zugleich den Ton an für eine höchst unheilige Behandlung von Gegenständen, die bisher eine Art Bildungsglaube vor Verunglimpfungen sicherer geschützt hatte als der religiöse Glaube die Lehren der Kirche."[5] To be sure, this is the extent of Schneider's elaboration concerning Wieland and the travesty. Humor, irony, and tact—qualities with which Wieland was abundantly endowed—are paramount to a travesty of high artistic niveau. While the reader perceives the subtle presence of his cosmopolitanism in many of his literary products, the travesty offers an ideal outlet, for it involves the humorous refashioning of existing works or elements thereof, and, in some cases, refinement of inferior ones. Wieland proved to be equal to the challenge: he was able to invest characters and situations with a comic touch without distorting them to the level of caricature, or subtly to deemphasize the aura of time-honored, traditionally revered institutions without debasing them in the manner of earlier parodistic products. His gentle, humorous skepticism was instrumental in engendering a new brand of travesty. At the same time Wieland rendered a valuable service to German literature as a whole when one considers the relative paucity of humorous works. His humor is particularly effective when it is dispensed with a bit of philosophy, censure, or advice, for it tends to coat and lighten any measure of didacticism peculiar to the travesty.

In order to arrive at a valid definition of the term "travesty" I have consulted numerous sources with the ultimate realization that semantic problems inherent in the term, and its apparent kinship with the related "parody" seem to preclude a precise delimitation.

The *Deutsches Wörterbuch* compiled by Jacob and Wilhelm Grimm (Leipzig, 1890), p. 1567, defines *Travestie* as a genre differing from the parody, thus a "komische, meist satirische wirkung erstrebende dichtungsgattung, im 18. jh. aus gleichbed. engl. *travesty* entlehnt..., das im 17. jh. aus dem partic. des französ. verbums *travestir*..., veranlasst durch Scarrons *Virgile travesty* (1648), gebildet wurde: die travestie ist das entgegengesetzte von parodie; dort wird der inhalt beibehalten, aber durch eine verdrehte behandlung ins lächerliche gewandt (bei der parodie umgekehrt)." In the *Reallexikon der deutschen Literaturgeschichte*, Vol. III (Berlin, 1966), 12-72, the authors make little distinction between the two terms, but rather refer the reader to *Parodie* for an extensive elaboration. While agreeing that in theory a technical difference exists, the authors maintain that in practice, parody and travesty are often! fused (13). The *Reallexikon* holds that travesty achieves its comic effect through the retention of the original plot in an incongruous form. The *Kleines literarisches Lexikon*, ed. Wolfgang Kayser, Vol. I (Bern, München, 1961), 173-174, lists *Parodie* and *Travestie* in one rubric, pointing out not only traits common to both but also differences between the two:

Gemeinsam ist den beiden Begriffen: Verspottung eines dichterischen Werkes durch Erzeugen einer komischen Spannung zwischen der Gestaltung u. dem Gestalteten. Ihr Sinn liegt in folgendem: sie wollen entweder auf Schwächen des Werkes hinweisen u. damit durch Offenbarung der Unzulänglichkeit auch des Großen tiefere Komik erzeugen, oder sie entspringen reiner komischer Gestaltungslust oder sie dienen dem Angriff u. der Kritik. Demnach kann man komische, kritische u. polemische P.n u. T.n unterscheiden. Der Unterschied zwischen beiden besteht darin: P. beläßt die Form der verspotteten Dichtung, ändert aber den Inhalt, der nun zur Form nicht mehr paßt; T. beläßt den Inhalt, gibt ihm aber eine andre, unpassende Form. Beide Arten können episch, dramatisch, ja auch lyrisch sein. Der Grad der Verspottung steht zwischen den Grenzfällen des harmlosen Spiels u. der ätzenden Schmähung. ...Alle lit. Richtungen u. Werke können parodiert u. travestiert werden, auch das größte....

A Glossary of Literary Terms, revised by M. H. Abrams (New York, 1957), pp. 9-10, maintains that "'Burlesque,' 'parody,' 'caricature,' and 'travesty' are often used interchangeably, but to equate the terms in this way is to surrender very useful critical distinctions.... A *parody*, like the mock epic, is also a form of high burlesque, but it derides, not its subject, but a particular literary work or style, by imitating its features and applying them to trivial or grossly discordant materials... the *travesty*, mocks a specific work by treating its lofty subject in grotesquely extravagant or lowly terms...." Gero von Wilpert in his *Sachwörterbuch der Literatur* (Stuttgart, 1959), p. 653, distinguishes sharply between the *Travestie* and the *Parodie*. As common to both he cites the comic effect achieved through the discrepancy between form and content, and their respective dependence upon a model; furthermore, both share a common purpose—either to underscore the weaknesses or shortcomings of a model, or to direct a verbal attack against an author and his creation in order to expose them to ridicule or simply to subject an existing work to comic variation for the sheer pleasure of it. Travesty, a satirical derision of a serious literary work, in contrast to parody, retains the plot but changes the form of its model. It may be applied to all genres—epic, drama, and lyric poetry. Wilpert makes the point that travesty, as a rule, is more harmless than the parody, and generally serves the purpose of pure amusement rather than involvement in literary feuds. Robert Petsch in his work *Wesen und Formen der Erzählung* (Halle/Saale, 1934), p. 280, observes that the ridiculous is but a step away from the sublime where exaggeration of human values is at work, as is the case, for example, in the heroic epic. Any transgression of plausible boundaries of human potential, however noble the motive, invites our repulsion, maintains Petsch. It seems that this observation would be especially à propos of a skeptic with a penchant for irony, such as Wieland. Two kinds of misshapen genres, Petsch continues, were the natural consequence of the exaggerated epic sublimity. Of these two, the "bösartige Travestie" receives a rather pejorative appraisal as a "Verbiegung des Heroischen ins Gespreizte, des Bewunderungswürdigen ins Verlogene, des Edlen ins Versteckt-Gemeine, mitsamt der Betonung alles Niedrigen und allzu Menschlichen. Auch hier liegt eine Übersteigerung der Wirklichkeit vor, nur nach der anderen Seite.... Die harmlosere Art ist die 'Parodie,'... welche den hohen Ton des Epos auf Gegenstände von geringer Bedeutung anwendet...."

Friedrich W. Ebeling in his work *Geschichte der komischen Literatur in Deutschland während der 2. Hälfte des 18. Jahrhunderts*, Vol. III (Leipzig, 1869), 448, concedes that the *parody* shares the form with its model while the *travesty* aims occasionally at distorting the serious content of a poetic work through deliberate alteration of the format.

In his article "Parodie, Travestie und Pastische. Zur Geschichte von Wort und Sache," *Germanisch-Romanische Monatsschrift*, XV (April 1965), 150-176, Wido Hempel laments the inconsistency in the definition of the terms involved. He notes that, used as verbs, both terms, *parodieren*, and *travestieren* may be encountered in German usage. The noun, *die Travestie*, first appeared in German in the eighteenth century, according to Hempel (*cf.* p. 4), while its English derivative, *the travesty*, has been proven to have first occurred in 1674, borrowed from the French verb *travestir*. Interestingly, neither the French nor the Italian has noun equivalents phonetically corresponding to the English *travesty* and the German *Travestie*, *i.e.*, no such nouns as the French *la travestie* or the Italian *la travestia* exist; instead, these terms are *travestissement*, and *travestimento*, respectively. The Italian verb *travestire* has occurred in Machiavelli, its participle *travestito* can be found in Boccaccio. Montaigne used the French equivalent for the verb borrowed from the Italian. In its original meaning, the term means 'mask' or 'disguise,' and is also used as a reflexive verb. The parody, Hempel proceeds, is two millenia older than the travesty, having been in vogue in Greece even prior to the coinage of the word. The Greek *parodia* meant an innovation in epic technique of recitation, involving metric considerations. The nature of the parody presupposes familiarization on the part of the audience with the model, *i.e.*, the work which is being parodied. Furthermore, the parody may be concerned with the realms of literature or music. Travesty is possible in literature, and in the fine arts, and is more loosely used. In general, the aim of the travesty is the conversion of sublime expression into comic effect. Ernst Wasserzieher, in *Woher? Ableitendes Wörterbuch der deutschen Sprache* (Bonn, 1959), p. 403, defines travesty as "scherzhafte od. spöttische Umgestaltung e. Gedichtes, lt. *trans* über, hinaus, *vestis* Kleid, also eig. Umkleidung, s. Weste, Investitur." *Der Sprachbrockhaus* (Wiesbaden, 1959), p. 699, gives *Travestie* as "scherzhafte, oft verhöhnende Umdichtung einer ernsten Dichtung." *Der große Brockhaus*, Vol. XI of 23 vols. (Wiesbaden, 1957), 606, lists as its definition for 'travesty' "satirische Dichtungsart, die ein anderes Literaturwerk dadurch verspottet, daß sie im Gegensatz zur Parodie den Inhalt beibehält, ihm aber eine andere, nicht gemäße Form gibt...."

In spite of the existing discrepancies in nomenclature and admittedly confusing distinction, it is clearly apparent that

Wieland favored the technique of following the basic plot outlines of his sources while altering the manner of presentation; for example, adapting prose works into verse narratives. This study will, therefore, examine chiefly those works which constitute travesties according to the method just set forth. It will also investigate more or less dominant elements of the travesty within the context of works which might be classified as travesties only in the wider sense of the term, or not so at all, in order to round out the inquiry.

PART I

THE THEORY

CHAPTER I

THE STATE OF THE TRAVESTY IN GERMAN LITERATURE BEFORE WIELAND

When in the Introduction to this study I made the point that the word *Travestie* first appeared in the German language in the eighteenth century, I meant literally the word. The form itself existed, of course, long before it was named, as generally, the product precedes the label. In this chapter, I may not be able to maintain consistently a sharp distinction between the classifications of parody, and travesty as outlined in the Introduction because first, there are indeed few pure travesties, and secondly, some traits common to both forms do manifest themselves. My chronological presentation up to Wieland will encompass trends or works which appear to fall into the category of my consideration, *i.e.*, into the province of satire, and which—by contrast—will let Wieland's contribution appear all the more impressive.

In his work, *The Anatomy of Satire* (Princeton, 1962), Gilbert Highet indeed treats parody, as well as mimicry, as an example of satire; to be sure, one of its most delightful forms which differs from distortion and imitation by its intention and its effect (p. 67). Another author, David Worcester in his book, *The Art of Satire* (Cambridge, Massachusetts, 1949), conceives of the invective, the burlesque, and various forms of irony as instruments of satirical criticism in which the emotion is controlled, the blow softened through indirect approach (p. 17).

If one consults a reference work on the history of German literature or literary terms, one invariably observes the preponderance of examples in the rubric of parody or travesty as dating from Romanticism. Might one credit the celebrated ingredient of Romantic irony, the wit of the age, and the fact that more models were available to be travestied? One also notes the extreme paucity of travesties in German literature of the Middle Ages. It is difficult to imagine that medieval erudites had lacked a penchant for the travesty, judging especially from the rich evidence of caricature—another art form which intentionally exaggerates, distorting the proportions of an object to a satirical end, often with a didactic purpose. Extant sculptures and woodcuts in great cathedrals and other public buildings eloquently attest to an active interest in the art of grotesque depiction. The language of the fine arts appeals through its universality. A higher level of abstraction involves verbal communication of ideas. Parodistic expression is traditionally held to be a preoccupation of keen minds with a critical attitude of their environment and their contemporaries, but above all, an intellectual exercise of the educated. Small wonder that medieval German travesties were so few in an age when the language of the learned strata was Latin. Indeed, the wealth of more or less sophisticated contributions by clerics and *vagi* bespeaks medieval man's attitude toward the genre—his delight in indulging in this somewhat irreverent pastime hardly becoming the clerics' station. There is evidence of all manner of parodistic sacrilege: literary and dramatic profanation of spiritual themes, deliberate mingling of religious hymns with mundane tunes of current popularity, disparaging adaptations of the text of parts of the mass; in short, an alarming quantity of travesties injurious to the Church and her tenets (*cf. Reallexikon*, III, 16, 62-63).

The development of the vernacular into a literary language was a slow process. Even in the late parodistic product of the Middle Ages on German soil, the brilliant *epistolae virorum obscurorum*, wit and biting irony find expression in Latin. The sparse use of the German language in early medieval literature does not yield any evidence of parody or travesty. During the Golden Age of Middle High German poetry—especially in the epic—a few sarcastically or critically colored references to other poets or works occur; but such manifestations, for example, certain allusions to Reinmar by Walther von der Vogelweide, or Gottfried von Straßburg's criticism of Wolfram von Eschenbach as a "vindaere wilder Maere" (Tristan's *Schwertleite*), surely bear no resemblance to travesty. With the decline of *Minnedichtung*, beginning with Neidhart von Reuenthal, and the rise of the bourgeois spirit, the German parody—perhaps more than the travesty—was coming into its own on the fertile soil of an age of transition in which the old tradition was gradually giving way to a new order. One perceives the ironic, drastic degradation of such exalted institutions as *hohe minne*, courtly and even popular epic (*e.g.*, *Das Nibelungenlied*), and chivalrous society. The deterioration of formerly aspired high ideals is illustrated frequently through an incongruous form of expression, such as the rustic *Tanzdichtung*. Certainly, one can ascribe strong parodistic tendencies to Wernher der Gartenaere's didactic *Meier Helmbrecht*, and, in a wider sense, might one not term this work a travesty on decaying chivalry? In Heinrich Wittenweiler's *Der Ring* (ca. 1400), ribald peasant motifs and tone are carried *ad absurdum*, conveying sharp dissonance with its epic form. Sebastian Brant's *Das Narrenschiff* (1494), generally labeled a moral satire in allegorical frame, censures human foibles from poor table manners to the seven mortal sins. By its portrayal of men as fools it might be accepted as a parody on a segment of humanity, but in a strict sense it could not be called a parody or a travesty—even though the idea of neither the ship nor the fool in literature was original with Brant; his form is no longer the epic but rather a loosely woven sequence of sermons laced with irony and homespun humor, intended to entertain while being instructive. Among the Humanists, for example, Heinrich Bebel (1472-1518), and Nicodemus Frischlin (1547-1590), artful Latin *facetiae* later gave rise to the German *Schwankliteratur*, an immensely popular, if intellectually less demanding, brand of moral satire to a didactic end.

In the spirit of Desiderius Erasmus' *Laus stultitiae* (1508), the didactic practice of ironic praise was growing in prominence, as seen, for example, in Johann Fischart's *Podagrammatisch Trostbüchlein* (1577).

The German language, too, was now beginning to lend itself to parodistic profanation of religious themes. Adapted from Marian salutatory invocations, a colorful variety of toasts (*Trunksprüche*) came into vogue, especially with the rise of the universities, and was perpetuated through traveling scholars, minstrels, journeymen, and mercenaries (*cf.* Johann Fischart's *Geschichtklitterung*, Chapter 3, where a *Trunkenlitanei* occurs).

An increasing realism fostered the parodistic animal fable, as indicated by such titles of some sixteenth-century exponents as Johann Fischart's *Die Flöhhaz* (1575), and Georg Rollenhagen's *Der Froschmeuseler* (1595), among others.

It is obvious that a powerful movement like the Reformation cultivated the parody and the travesty, and more so the sharper satire on all levels of sophistication, as an effective polemic weapon. Monastic statutes, ecclesiastical decrees, papal bulls, as well as documents and letters involving civil authorities and mundane institutions were unmercifully parodied. Hardly a guild or class of society escaped profanation to some degree (*cf.* litany against judicial officials, peasant catechism, peasant declension, defamatory incantations on all guilds and classes). There is evidence of "satanic" letters adapted from princely decrees and directed to the papal curia, "The Passion of Doctor Martin Luther," in gospel style, and the recomposition of Protestant hymns. Thomas Murner in his *Die Gäuchmatt* (1515) achieved a parody on the cumbersome documentary style. Here, and in his other verse satires, *Die Narrenbeschwörung* (1512), and *Die Schelmenzunft* (1512), Murner continued Brant's tradition of *Narrenliteratur*. Friedrich Dedekind's *Grobianus* (1549), translated from the original Latin into German by Kaspar Scheidt (1557), coarsely parodied rules of etiquette, with a didactic implication, of course, while the popular calendar prophecies were being taken to task by contemporary wits. Fischart, as grotesque a satirist as a linguistic creative spirit, and probably the most imaginative mind in sixteenth century German literature, excelled in his parodistic efforts, for example, *Aller Praktik Großmutter* (1572), based mainly on François Rabelais's *Pantagrueline Prognosticatio* (1533). Fischart's most prominent satirical work is his *Affenteurliche vnd Ungeheurliche Geschichtschrift Vom Leben, rhaten vnd Thaten der for langen weilen Vollen wol beschraiten Helden vnd Herrn Grandgusier, Gargantoa vnd Pantagruel, Königen von Vtopien vnd Ninenreich* (1575) — the third edition introduced the title *Geschichtklitterung*, an adaptation of Rabelais's *Gargantua et Pantagruel* (1532-1564). It contains parodies of folk tunes, comic imitation of the fusion of German and Latin terms peculiar to the language of his day, a parody of the litany (*v. sup.*), and the like. A parody of the closing formula of the mass, for example, may be found in Fischart's *Die Wunderlichst Vnerhörtest Legend vnd Beschreibung Des Angeführten, Quartirten, Gevierten vnd Vierekkechten Vierhörnigen Hütleins*, more commonly known as *Das Jesuiterhütlein* (1580).

The Baroque age offers a limited share of true travesties — mostly adaptations into low German via France of the works of Catullus, Horace, and Vergil. Outside of German literature, Vergil's *Aeneid* had been travestied by Giovanni Battista Lolli, Paul Scarron, Jacques Moreau, John Dryden, among others. Individual parodistic criticism of sixteenth century poetic coarseness, for example, the dominant use of the doggerel, is plentiful; Andreas Gryphius' scorn in his *Absurda Comica oder Herr Peter Squentz* (1657) might be cited in this connection. On the other hand, the extreme purism of the *Sprachgesellschaften*, and the pedantry on the part of certain contemporary poets were a welcome object of literary ridicule, *e.g.*, in Andreas Gryphius' *Horribilicribrifax* (1663), or in Christian Weise's *Lustspiel von einer zweifachen Poetenzunft* (1680). As a staunch "convert" to the anti-*Schwulst* camp, Christian Wernicke injected many of his epigrams with quotations parodied from bombastic creations by Christian Hofmann von Hofmannswaldau, and Daniel Kasper von Lohenstein.

The eighteenth century gave rise to significant developments which have determined the views concerning the nature and artistic value of parodistic literary products almost to our times (*cf. Reallexikon*, III, 18). Among the pertinent criteria are the growing prevalence of the "critical parody" in the service of literary feuds (*v. infra*), and the emergence of the travesty as a pleasurable literary exercise with lesser parodistic intent. The spirit of the age was receptive to Wieland's contribution, and his talent, on the other hand, complemented the trend of the time.

The first half of the eighteenth century in German literature is characterized prominently by the ideological feud of two leading literary schools, Leipzig, *i.e.*, Johann Christoph Gottsched and his followers, Schönaich, Triller, and Schwabe among them, versus Zürich, *i.e.*, Johann Jakob Bodmer and Johann Jakob Breitinger, and their camp. In the bitter controversy, parodistic material, too, was pressed into the service by both sides. The Swiss reacted with a venomous parody to the publication of an anthology of insipid fables and moralistic poems by Daniel Stoppe, a member of the Leipzig circle (*Neue Fabeln oder moralische Gedichte*, Leipzig, 1738, 1740). Although reciprocation by the opposition was prompt, it appears that the Swiss and their sympathizers eventually emerged as the superior contestants in the arena of parodistic effort. While parody and travesty at that stage were prone to mock individual works or their authors, or both, they actually became factors contributory to the discipline of literary criticism which began to flourish in the eighteenth century (*cf. Reallexikon*, III, 43).

Albrecht von Haller, and Friedrich Gottlieb Klopstock's odes have also been subjected to a number of parodistic treatments. Johann Elias Schlegel's *Canut* (1746) was parodied by J. F. von Cronegk, Gottsched's *Der sterbende Cato* (1732) was mocked by an anonymous author who retained but cleverly reinterpreted the dialogue. *Polytimet* (1760) is the title of a parody of Gotthold Ephraim Lessing's *Philotas* (1759) by Bodmer. Heinrich Wilhelm von Gerstenberg, having parodied Bodmer's style in one of his *Schleswig* letters, received in reciprocation an unpublished parody (ca. 1769) on his *Ugolino* (1768). Matthias Claudius' *Wandsbeck* of 1774 contains a burlesque treatment of the pathetic scene in Gerstenberg's *Ugolino*. A flippant reference by Bürger to that tragedy can be found in the *Göttinger Musen-Almanach* of 1777.[1] Johann

Heinrich Voß, and Wieland, on the occasion of the latter's *Alceste*, were also attacked through parodies by Bodmer.

Among the Anacreontic poets, jocular parodies and travesties outdid the more or less vitriolic products which served polemic ends—of religious, ideological, literary or whatever description. Comic imitations of works by Horace, Vergil, and Ovid, among the classical authors, and of their own contemporaries were perpetuated by Johann Wilhelm von Gleim, Ewald von Kleist, Ludwig Hölty, Friedrich von Hagedorn, Johann Heinrich Voß, Gottfried August Bürger, among others.

The increasing popularity of the comic epic toward the end of the eighteenth century undoubtedly gave rise to a growing interest in the travesty, a genre somewhat akin to that of the comic epic. A genuine contribution was *Leben und Taten des teuren Helden Aeneas* (1771) by J. B. Michaelis, a theater writer. This promising travesty—left fragmentary by the author's death—was inadequately continued by F. Berkhan (1779). Yet, inspired by this work, Aloys Blumauer created his *Aeneis* (1784-1788) which achieves its effect mainly through a series of anachronistic situations, and which has been recognized as one of the most brilliant, sparklingly witty contributions to the genre, although Friedrich von Schiller and others have sharply criticized its frivolity. While denying any influence of Paul Scarron's *Le Virgile travesti en vers burlesques* (1648-1652), he did admit being inspired by Wieland.[2] In his work, Blumauer, a champion of the Austrian Enlightenment, combats the evils of political and religious tyranny, ignorance, and superstition, by way of a cleverly irreverent scrutiny of the past, just as Wieland had done before him; to be sure, Wieland's criticism was not rarely pointed against the contemporary scene. Another Austrian, Johann Baptist von Alxinger authored *Rittergedichte* in the manner of Wieland's *Oberon*, and mock epics related in spirit and style to that of Blumauer.[3] A host of imitations followed in the wake of Blumauer's *Aeneis* which continued to enjoy enormous popularity, especially in the literary circles of Vienna to the days of the *Wiener Volksstück*.

Parody and travesty were the essential literary means of retaliation against the spreading "epidemic" of *Empfindsamkeit*. In this spirit, Johann Karl Musäus directed his *Grandison II oder die Geschichte des Herrn von N. in Briefen entworfen* (1760-1762), later revised under the title *Der deutsche Grandison. Auch eine Familiengeschichte* (1778-1779), chiefly against the imitators of Richardson.

Blumauer and Georg Christoph Lichtenberg took Bürger to task. By way of the travesty, Friedrich Nicolai was ridiculing the increasing inclination for popular (*volkstümlich*) expression, particularly through the *Volkslied*. His *Die Freuden des jungen Werthers* (1775) inflamed Goethe's wrath, and led to the latter's *Anektode* [sic] *zu den Freuden des jungen Werther* (published Leipzig, 1862), plus several poems deriding Nicolai. The latter enraged the Romanticists by incorporating scornful adaptations of some of Friedrich Schlegel's fragments in his novel *Vertraute Briefe von Adelheid B* an ihre Freundin Julie S** (1799). Ludwig Tieck, among other Romanticists, reciprocated with parodistic references in his *Prinz Zerbino* (1799).

The anti-Wieland play *Götter, Helden und Wieland* (1774), is neither a parody nor a travesty, technically speaking, but rather a satire against Wieland and his works, mostly *Alceste*, which Goethe scorned at the time. He composed the "Farce" on an impulse and permitted its publication, although he later regretted his rashness.[4]

At a time of such prolific literary production few authors indeed remained immune from some type of satirical attack. In the following chapter I shall investigate Wieland's attitude toward the genre of the travesty, his ironic inclination coupled with a propensity for borrowing his plots, especially from foreign sources. Above all, I shall inquire into the nature of his contribution to the genre.

The present chapter yields the conclusion that from the inception of written tradition in German literature, pure travesty is rare, indeed. Even though I have shown parodistic tendencies *en masse*, there is limited evidence up to Wieland of the occurrence of the travesty in the meaning which I outlined in the Introduction. Moreover, I demonstrated the fact that the parodies or travesties examined were used predominantly as polemic or didactic tools directed against an individual, society, or a literary school for the purpose of effrontery, ridicule, or in reciprocation thereof. The *prodesse* portion of Horace's famous dictum, "aut prodesse... aut delectare," as the function of poets, might be said to have had the upper hand until the later eighteenth century when parody and travesty became a conscious exercise of the wit to other than a purely utilitarian end. Wieland had created most of his travesties before 1780. How he ameliorated the status of a hitherto trivial genre, lent it aesthetic justification, and influenced its further development into modern times is the object of my analysis in the following chapter.

CHAPTER II

WIELAND'S APPROACH TO THE TRAVESTY: HIS SATIRICAL PENCHANT

The thoughtful reader or critic of Wieland's work is aware of the dual intention in the poet's creations: to instruct while entertaining. In many facets, indeed, in a spectrum of examples a happy blend of his subtle didactic message, his criticism, and his humor can be perceived—tempered, of course, according to the exigencies of any given literary situation.

His background, his personal makeup, his inclinations, and the limitations of his talent, but certainly environmental conditioning factors, and the taste of his time may be cited as agents contributing to Wieland's extraordinary parodistic gift.

Christoph Martin Wieland lived through a number of dominant literary epochs. A child of the *Aufklärung*, he underwent a personal metamorphosis from his period of religious fervor influenced by Pietism, through the elegance, grace, wit, and skepticism of the Rococo which is an expression of the Enlightenment. Undaunted by the excesses of the *Sturm und Drang* phase, he may be considered as a pioneer of Classicism, and indeed, of Romanticism, even though the latter school sought to damage Wieland's literary stature, and ultimately succeeded in disseminating the message derogatory to his fame. Wieland is remarkable in having never completely embraced any one literary movement, but rather having remained in his own individual tracks. His cosmopolitanism was recognized and lauded by his admirers, but censured by his critics (*cf*. Albert Fuchs, *Les Apports français dans l'Oeuvre de Wieland de 1772 à 1789*. Paris, 1934). Wieland, they maintained, had failed to commit himself consistently to the precepts of any one literary school: as an imitator of the French and their ways, he was branded a frivolous *Tugendverderber* and *Jugendverführer*.[1]

The Romanticists, on the other hand, condemned Wieland as a surviving relic—but apparently one of sufficiently prominent stature—the relic of an age to which their philosophy was diametrically opposed.[2] The intensity of the Romantic feud with Wieland represents something of a phenomenon in itself when one considers the numerous striking parallels that form common denominators for Wieland and the Romantic school, namely: Wieland's irony, his penchant for the fragmentary, his interest in the past and its literature, in the fairy tale, and in Shakespeare whose almost complete dramatic works he made accessible to German audiences through his prose translations (1762-1766), thereby laying the groundwork or lending impetus for later, better translations.

Among the major shortcomings, as they saw them, Wieland's prosecutors underscored his lack of profundity, his exaggerated Epicurean sensuality, with occasional evidence of overt immorality. Lessing in his *8. Literaturbrief* takes exception to Wieland's "affectirte Tiefsinnigkeiten,...profane Allusionen."[3] In his *13. Literaturbrief*, dated February 1, 1759, he has these critical words for Wieland: "Allein was geht Herr Wielanden das Gründliche an? Er ist ein erklärter Feind von allem, was einige Anstrengung des Verstandes erfordert...."[4] But playful, witty eroticism, and a degree of superficiality are a trademark of the Rococo whose main representative in Germany Wieland was. In his article "Wieland and Sceptical Rationalism," I. S. Stamm credits the poet with a "subtle depth of superficiality," while agreeing that "Wieland's sense of the deep was not strong or rich enough to give dramatic, let alone mythic, quality to his expression. Yet in his urbane way he knew well enough what was in the world around and beneath man, so that his superficiality, like that of the Rococo in general may suggest a special quality of significance."[5]

Ermatinger conceives of the "Verhältnis von Tugend und Genuß, Geist und Sinnlichkeit..." as the basic problem of Wieland's age. Indeed, Wieland himself war so beschaffen, daß er ein sehr zärtliches Gemüt mit einem klaren Verstande verband. Es dauerte geraume Zeit, ehe er sich durch die Wirrnisse... hindurch gekämpft hatte zu der Ironie eines lächelnden, sowohl verstandesklaren als gemütswarmen Darüberstehens.... Diese Beweglichkeit ist der Grund seiner Persönlichkeit.... Sicherlich wirkte Wielands Beweglichkeit sehr oft nur auf der Oberfläche der Dinge, denen er gerade seine Liebe schenkte, und wenn man ihn etwa den deutschen Voltaire genannt hat, so ist zu sagen, daß Wieland viel zu weich und verbindlich war, als daß er jenen unweigerlichen Ernst, jene unerbittliche Schärfe und diabolische Bosheit aufgebracht hätte, die Voltaire in den Fragen an den Tag legte, in welchen er keinen Spaß verstand—Wieland verstand nur zuviel Spaß, und er war gutmütiger als Voltaire.[6]

Literary products in the satirical vein are often associated with a stigma of virulence. Wieland's *Heiterkeit*, however, moderated the passions, allowing for the intermingling of jest with earnest through occasional sarcasm but never by means of dejection, bitterness, or cynicism. The duchess Anna Amalia, Wieland's benefactress and friend, attested to his amiable personality and to the degree of *Menschenkenntnis* demonstrated in his works, although at the time of his release from public duties at Weimar she had reason to conclude that Wieland's actual knowledge of the human psyche was less intimate when it came to his private contacts. She said, "Er ist ein Mann von gefühlvollem Herzen und ehrenwerter Gesinnung; aber ein schwacher Enthusiast, viel Eitelkeit und Eigenliebe; ich erkenne leider zu spät, daß er nicht gemacht ist für die Stellung, in der er sich befindet; er ist zu schwärmerisch für die jungen Leute, zu schwach, um ihnen die Spitze zu bieten, und zu unvorsichtig, in seiner Lebhaftigkeit hat er das Herz auf der Zunge; wenn er sich verfehlt, so ist das mehr aus Schwachheit als aus bösem Willen; so sehr er durch seine Schriften gezeigt hat, daß er das menschliche Herz im allgemeinen kennt, so wenig kennt er das einzelne Herz und die

Individuen..." (quoted by Sengle, pp. 277-278). From the comments of Bodmer, Herder, Goethe, Madame de Staël, and other notable contemporaries, as well as the presentations of his biographer and friend, J. G. Gruber, the editor of *C. M. Wielands sämmtliche Werke* (Leipzig: Göschen, 1824-1828), Sengle evolves the image of an enlightened cosmopolite—in spite of his pronounced, genuine interest in simple domestic joys in the circle of his large family—a *littérateur*, translator, educator, philosopher, and last but not least, a pleasant *causeur*. This "anmutige Plauderton" (Schneider, p. 293) is evident throughout many of his works, even during philosophical elaborations in more demanding genres, such as the novel, for example *Agathon*. But is not the tone, as an aspect of style, a manifestation of *Heiterkeit*? This intangible spirit so widely and perhaps vaguely associated with the eighteenth century seeks a meeting point between excessive exuberance and reservation. It is an articulation of philosophical optimism, even though a dose of wisely balanced, cautious pessimism, or at best, some degree of fatalism, may be obscured behind the layer of smiling optimism. *Heiterkeit*, then, may be viewed as a compromise, a mood or *Seelenzustand* of optimum balance—a balance between the factors of pleasure and displeasure (or discord in any form). Moderation in the expectation of the degree of pleasure will serve to reduce the incidence of disappointment, that is, disturbance, and certainly, of any suffering which may ensue from self-induced causes. This very mood pervades Wieland's "reizende Philosophie." It is the clever, charming Musarion who endorses the harmony of the opposing concepts so descriptive of Wieland's peculiar duality between sensuality and intellect, Epicureism and Stoicism, idealism and realism: "...Genießest wenn du kannst, und leidest wenn du mußt..." (XII, 19). Nevertheless, his sanguine temperament seems to dominate. It is the ideal of *Heiterkeit* which tempers passions and provides a milieu, as it were, for many of Wieland's satirical narratives, thereby taking the harshness out of the intended gibe.

The quest for balance may also be seen in Wieland's feeling toward enthusiasm which in itself affords a glimpse into his problematic personality. He distinguished between enthusiasm ("wehe dem, dem keine Nerven dazu schwingen!", LII, 186), and mere *Schwärmerei*, a "...Zauberzustand einer Menschenseele, wo sie,... ihre eignen ungeheuersten Einbildungen für wirkliche Empfindungen hält; gar als feste, göttliche Offenbarungen verehret und als solche verehrt wissen will" (LII, 186). In this spirit he continues: "Immer Enthusiast seyn, ist nicht gut; und nicht gut, immer kaltblütiger Philosoph seyn. Jedes an Ort und Stelle zu seyn, das ist gut. Dieß lehrt der Kopf, jenes das Herz. Reißt nicht Eins weg, sondern zeigt mit beiden, wie sie zum großen Zweck des Lebens harmoniren. Wirft der Enthusiast immer und alle Regeln weg; er thut Unrecht" (LII, 187). It is *Schwärmerei*, that is, uncontrolled enthusiasm, prejudice, superstition, and gullibility which Wieland takes to task, along with the fairy hierarchy, in his adventure novel *Die Abenteuer des Don Sylvio von Rosalva*. Nevertheless, he tolerated these emotions—in optimum measure—for their positive function: "...beyde [Schwärmerey und Aberglaube] bringen viel Gutes hervor; die Schwärmerey macht glänzende, kühne und unternehmende Geister, der Aberglaube zahme, geduldige, förmliche Thiere, die ...für alles ihre Vorschrift haben, von der sie nicht abweichen dürfen. Allein ... ist es doch jederzeit für sehr nöthig und heilsam geachtet worden, über jene Triebfeder der großen Leidenschaften, und über diese plumpe *vis inertiae* der menschlichen Natur sich lustig zu machen. Der Scherz und die Ironie sind nebst dem ordentlichen Gebrauch der fünf Sinne immer für das beste Mittel gegen die Ausschweifungen von beyden angesehen worden...."[7]

The middle-of-the-road approach which he advocates and seems to embrace himself does not, however, suggest complacency. Instead, it is a sign of growing maturity and of a mellowing process through thoughtful resignation or adjustment to existing conditions. This attitude provided Wieland with a conciliatory spirit and ultimately formulated his *humanitas*. The many "stations" of his intellectual development are, to be sure, marked by vacillations between disappointments, pessimism, and hedonistic *Diesseitsfreudigkeit*.

These extremes, experienced and eventually overcome, lend Wieland's work tensile quality. One worthwhile, observable symptom resulting from these modulations is irony, perhaps a device for the escape from the passions. Wieland's skepticism, his sophisticated wit, and the polished elegance of his expression infused his travesties with the ingredient basic, yet hitherto rare in the genre. While he acknowledged occasional prolixity and the lack of the "... Kunst, mit wenigem viel zu sagen," his urbane style nevertheless contributed immeasurably to the development of his ideas in the best manner of a great ironist (*DB*, II, 149). Influenced by the examples of Fielding and Sterne, he establishes and maintains contact with his audience, involving it through polite address, rhetorical question, and occasional pertinent reference. This idiosyncrasy of style, to be sure, retards the action but, on the other hand, it charmingly enhances the presentation. Wieland seems to resort to deliberate indirectness for effect. His reticence is rooted in tact urged by personal inclination and the expectations of his contemporaries in an age of polite *Gefühlskultur*. Intention and capability of weaving civility and poise into the fabric of the travesty represent decidedly a major innovation and a *tour de force* on Wieland's part. Not only did his assiduous avoidance of crassness endear him to his "gentle" readers, whose urbanity he sought to further; it also facilitated presentation of subjects which border on the risqué. Wieland possessed the unique gift of mitigating the notoriety of some of his borrowed plots. Where decorum demanded it, he was given to indicate delicately rather than to state. In the fashion of the Rococo *je ne sais quoi*, a spirit which knew how to hint, wink, and gesture, as it were, he was inclined discreetly to leave conclusions to his readers. When Eric Blackall in his work *The Emergence of German as a Literary Language 1700-1775* (Cambridge, 1959), pp. 410 ff., credits Wieland with the mastery of the *pointe*, I feel that this praise is due especially in consideration of the travesty where not rarely "...something sounding grand turns out to be something quite ordinary. Things are not what they seem to be" (Blackall, p. 420). The dash becomes almost a mark of artistic refinement at the hands of Wieland; he is using it as an indication of conscious reflection, like a rest employed in a musical score—not only for balance, but also for pausing momentarily before the resolution, as if to cogitate on the completion of the thought, or to give it a capricious twist into another direction.

His keen insight and social discernment endowed him with the touch to create moods, surely a sensitive and aesthetic contribution to the realm of the travesty. To this satirical genre he lent an entire register of sentiments, from drastic candor (*cf. Kombabus*), to grotesqueness (*cf. Schach Lolo*), to tenderness (*cf.* the island episode in *Oberon*)—an attribute not ordinarily associated with the travesty. All these nuances Wieland blended "... mit verführerischem Reiz, gleichsam tuschelnd und mit den Augen zwinkernd, kurz in jener nur diskret andeutenden Art, die mit der Zugkraft des Halbverhüllten wirkt und unstreitig eine technische Meisterleistung des ... Rokoko ist."[8] We perceive the demarcation between genuine and simulated sentiments which Wieland achieved through such stylistic devices as circumlocution, malapropism, mock-pedantry, and related rhetorical affectations.

In his efforts of balancing rationalism and empiricism he turned amateur psychologist. From his intimate familiarity with the human psyche he portrayed convincing, three-dimensional characters which in many instances resemble their models in name only, and who are anything but distortions. Even the negative portrayals (*cf.* the prototype of an Oriental potentate, *i.e.*, any absolute ruler)—Wieland's *forte*—usually confine themselves to criticism of mental and moral shortcomings rather than belaboring physical features.

His literary pursuit of truth and morality not infrequently finds an outlet in the travesty which is basically didactic. But Wieland's spirit is alien to a consistent, heavy didacticism, and constitutes much of the aesthetic appeal of his travesties. I conclude that he was less concerned with sublime issues of religion or political enlightenment or even virtue (*Tugend*) than with the harmony of head and heart, the aesthetic education of man, and the problems involving earthly human happiness.

While casting about for a suitable mold into which to pour the matter of his lighthearted travesties, Wieland repeatedly chose the fairy tale; that is to say, he fashioned usually rhymed, highly artistic verse narratives after existing tales in the fantastic genre, or he employed fairy paraphernalia in prose works. His contribution to this genre earned him a place as a refined stylist of *Kunstmärchen*. Wieland was aware of the enormous popularity of the fairy tale in an age which favored didacticism with a marvelous tinge. Keenly sensitive to the readers' taste as the editor of *Der Teutsche Merkur*, he commented as early as 1777: "Von allen Orten und Enden wird mir's zugerufen: mehr Märchen und mehr Rezensionen! Das Publikum will nichts anders, sagt man; wenigstens liest der große Haufe, an dem uns leider! am meisten gelegen seyn muß, nichts Liebers."[9] But it was more than mere indulgence of a popular vogue from a viewpoint of an enterprising *littérateur;* nor is it a coincidence that some of the best works of his mature peak period which Sengle labeled *humoristische Klassik* bear the markings of the marvelous. Wieland was aware of man's— even the enlightened person's—fascination with the world of the wonderful along with his concern for verisimilitude. This dual inclination seems to justify the fantastic guise which he so frequently employed. In the preface to the first part of the *Dschinnistan* collection, Wieland eloquently illustrated his sentiment concerning the fairy tale: "Es scheint seltsam, daß zwei so widersprechende Neigungen, als der Hang zum Wunderbaren und die Liebe zum Wahren, dem Menschen gleich natürlich, gleich wesentlich sein sollen; und doch ist es nicht anders."[10]

The skillful blend of the natural with illusion so as to fashion a "täuschendes Ganzes" to a didactic end constitutes an element of Wieland's novel aproach to the travesty. He, of course, welcomed the fairy tale with its fantastic appeal and more or less coated didacticism as a vehicle of criticism because this unpretentious genre affords unlimited possibilities of situations, settings, and characters in whose camouflage many a public person or trend may be taken to task with relative assurance of immunity. Besides, it provides an excellent means of presenting to the public certain truths which may otherwise be offensive, or of rendering certain forbidding subjects in such a manner as to make them aesthetically and popularly acceptable: "Man kann es nicht oft genug wiederholen: wer die Menschen von ihren Irrthümern und Unarten heilen will, muß seine Arzneien durch Beimischung irgend eines angenehmen Saftes oder geistigen Liquors angenehm zu machen wissen; und man unterrichtet und bessert sie nie gewisser, als wenn man das Ansehen hat, sie blos belustigen zu wollen" (Wieland, XXX, 7). This, too, is *Einkleidung*. Wieland's preoccupation with the supernatural is moderated through a liberal measure of skepticism. In his essay *Über den Hang der Menschen an Magie und Geistererscheinungen zu glauben* he muses: The more nature is known, explored, calculated, measured and weighed, the more wondrous, mysterious, and unknowable it appears to be. The infinite scene of its effects consumes our spirit which loses itself in a sea of miracles which, regardless of the state of scientific progress, leaves our limited imagination at a loss. "...Hierzu kommt noch ein andrer Umstand, der eine eben so natürliche Folge der Aufklärung ist, als er den Geistersehern günstig zu seyn scheint. Je weiter die Grenzen unsrer Kenntnisse hinaus gerückt werden, je mehr wir die unerschöpfliche Mannigfaltigkeit der Natur im Detail ihrer Werke kennen lernen; desto weiter dehnt sich auch der Kreis des Möglichen vor unsern Augen aus; und vielleicht ist es gerade der größte Naturforscher, der sich am wenigsten untersteht, irgend etwas, das nicht augenscheinlich in die Klasse der viereckigen Dreiecke gehört, für unmöglich zu erklären...." (XXXII, 132-133). He does not take his *Feerei* seriously. Indeed, one sees him poking good-natured fun at the entire hierarchy of the fairy realm and its paraphernalia (*cf. Die Abenteuer des Don Sylvio von Rosalva*). This reserved attitude toward his fantastic creatures and their world demonstrates his appraisal of their absurdity on the one hand, and their essential function within the framework of the fairy tale on the other. Wieland, whose tendency toward diminution (*cf.* the fantastic epyllion) appears to increase proportionately with his maturity, called on other less conspicuous genres, for example, the legend (*cf. Sixt und*

Clärchen), and the fable (*cf. Der Vogelsang*) which he successfully fused with factors requisite to the travesty.

Another idiosyncrasy which Wieland brought to the travesty is his propensity for the fragmentary which manifests itself in earlier works (*cf. Idris und Zenide*), and which by itself may constitute the expression of Wieland's irony, as Sengle maintains in his *Arbeiten zur deutschen Literatur 1750-1850*.[11] In the same source, Sengle appraises Wieland's attitude toward the traditional epic, and his resulting narrative technique—an artistic process which appears to be essential to the makeup of the travesty.

> Wieland weiß die Erzählung vortrefflich zu führen, er verliert sich weder ins Theoretisieren, noch ins Beschreiben, noch ins Träumen. Die Vorgänge sprechen durchaus für sich. Aber dazwischen muß auch der Erzähler immer wieder etwas sagen, was den Ernst der Vorgänge, die Wunder des Märchens, das Heldentum der Helden, die Verliebtheit der Liebenden, kurz die Schwere des Stoffes aufhebt. Die für Wielands Geschmack unerträgliche 'Monotonie,' die Stetigkeit und Objektivität des alten Epos sind ja Attribute seiner Übermenschlichkeit, seiner Monumentalität. Auch im Erzählstil und im Versmaß also, wie in der Menschendarstellung und im Format, zeigt sich die alles durchwaltende Tendenz auf *Verkleinerung* (Sengle, *Arbeiten*, p. 60).

Remarkably, Wieland transformed a majority of his prose sources into verse narratives—a rare and an equally demanding as aesthetically satisfying contribution to the realm of the travesty.

As stated, Wieland fostered refined sensuality. His own Epicurean frivolity, which he never denied once he had espoused it, and the demands imposed especially by his one-time influential sponsor, Count Stadion, account for some of The poet's choice of models. Wieland turned almost exclusively to foreign works from which he fashioned his travesties—his borrowings from the area of Germanic, specifically German, sources are negligible indeed. This imbalance in the distribution of source material may be due to the superior offerings by foreign literatures, to availability, and surely to the contemporary vogue of regarding French products as the *non plus ultra* in literary taste. Last but certainly not least, Wieland's own weakness for *Ausländerei*, his interests, and his taste for things foreign and exotic, played a considerable rôle in the selection of the sources for his travesties. He admittedly borrowed his plots, or elements thereof, from sources which appealed to him, and, like the poets of the courtly romances, fashioned his travesties on this basis, making no secret of his models.

The very nature of the travesty—that is, its demand for a model after which to fashion a new literary product—should absolve him. The possibility occurs to the present-day critic that Wieland's parodistic efforts were misunderstood. At any rate, his aesthetic contribution to the genre has been grossly underestimated. It is possible that the low and somewhat ignoble rank which the travesty occupies among literary genres has reflected upon Wieland as a chief exponent. In addition to its dependence upon a model, the traditional travesty is obligated by its function to degrade it to triviality or ridicule. Such negative inherent characteristics, and the lack of a truly dignified execution, have been responsible for the generally unfavorable aura surrounding the travesty. On the other hand, parodistic products—as I have shown—have had a long run, and will continue to enjoy popularity, even though they may be of lesser literary significance and profundity.

Wieland brought respectability to the travesty. By adding dignity to an ingredient rare in his native literature—humor—he marshaled the affection of some of his contemporary *literati*, notably Goethe, and he certainly merits our regard for an uncommon contribution.

PART II

WIELAND'S TRAVESTIES
AND THEIR SOURCES

CHAPTER III

THE NOVELS AND EPICS

A perusal of Wieland's early literary production readily yields the conclusion that his parodistic talent lay dormant for some time. Indeed, his Pietistic background, particularly the views of his strict father who opposed the precocious son's poetic furor, was hardly compatible with such literary "machinations." Yet, there is evidence of some early, if inconsequential, satire (*cf.* the poem *Von den Pygmäen*, satirizing *Rektor* Döll's wife, composed at twelve years of age). Such "practice pieces" which Wieland himself later destroyed, nevertheless constituted a part of the preparation for future, more sophisticated products in the parodistic vein. Moreover, a masterly niveau in this genre is predicated more upon the tact and superior discernment of a mature author than merely on the technical skill of a talented versifier.

His propensity for imitation, on the other hand, manifested itself early. So did his tendency toward didacticism. Through avid reading of Bayle, and later, of Fontenelle, d'Argens, and Voltaire, the youthful, devout Pietist experienced the initial impact of French skepticism and his resulting nearly agnostic outlook which was cause for temporary concern during the extreme stage of his first metamorphosis. The passionate study of Democritus, Leibniz, and Wolff, of ancient and modern tongues, and of critical works (*e.g.* Breitinger's *Critische Dichtkunst*) were to prepare him eminently to become an erudite poet befitting the age of the Enlightenment. His admiration for Brockes, Haller, Hagedorn, and Lucretius stimulated him to create didactic poems in their image and spirit. *Die Natur der Dinge* (1751), for example, is an imitation of Lucretius' *De rerum natura* of Wieland's Tübingen period. This formidably lengthy poem is an ambitious attempt, in alexandrine meter, at refuting its model, but it certainly does not aim at distorting it.

His tendency of earnestly emulating a model or even competing with it, free from parodistic intentions, was prevalent in his "formative" years. The influence of his reading (Gleim, Gellert, Lange, Milton, Vergil), the taste of the time, and probably the desire for personal success conditioned his choice of sources. There are echoes of Klopstock, only in more mundane, less elevated tones, in Wieland's *Lobgesang auf die Liebe* (1751), in spite of the enigmatic synthesis of seraphic and anacreontic paraphernalia. His *Hermann* (1751) makes us aware of a dutiful approach to the national epic which Bodmer, Wieland's future benefactor, was known to advocate. The *Zwölf moralische Briefe in Versen* (1752) have their model in the *Épîtres diverses sur des sujets différents* by Baron Georg Ludwig von Bar whom Gottsched revered as the foremost French poet in Germany.[1] In short, young Wieland on his road toward establishing a name for himself was eager for personal recognition and concerned about the critics' opinions. Following the manner of a renowned model held promise of approval, and, while the practice lacked originality, it afforded an opportunity for displaying his poetic powers.

His increasing propensity for "daintiness," that is, diminution of format, became evident in his *Anti-Ovid oder die Kunst zu lieben* (1752), as did his growing preoccupation with descriptive, lyrical poetry. Soon his superior potential in the lyric narrative evolved. The fugitive sensuousness of his lyric poems bears the mark of individuality—despite the unmistakable influence of noted ancient, and contemporary poets—and far excels his equally imitative odic efforts. Modest simplicity, indeed, lack of dimension and *pointe*, characterize the *Erzählungen* (1752) in the manner of Thomson and Rowe.

Wieland's coveted residence at Bodmer's house exposed him, to be sure, to the spirit of Homer, Milton, and Young.

Bodmer's extraordinary library, and the constant company of his prominent host afforded the young man remarkable opportunities for advancing his spiritual and social radius, but hardly an atmosphere conducive to fostering the creative mind, let alone a satirical leaning. Wieland was well aware of his advantages. He reciprocated by unconditionally abandoning his own literary inclinations in favor of his "master's" teachings. Along with his faddish devotion to Bodmer, he cultivated the hexameter, mostly within the framework of venerable, didactic themes. Yet, even under the gloomy mask, Wieland's narrative talent prevailed. To Bodmer's disappointment, his young dévoté never produced the grand epic which he, Bodmer, had foreseen. Eventual estrangement from Bodmer and increasing disillusionment lead to the beginning of Wieland's prose period—sober journalistic and pedagogic efforts. A surge of *Empfindsamkeit*, and an attempt in the dramatic genre (*Lady Johanna Gray*, 1758; *Clementina von Porretta*, 1760) mark the remainder of his Swiss episode. Sengle attaches considerable significance to Wieland's production of the sentimental tragedy at this particular stage of his literary evolution: the tearful melodrama—an incongruous, mixed genre which is devoid of the properties requisite to the genuine tragedy—he maintains, constitutes a preliminary step toward his satirico-humorous work (Sengle, pp. 114-115). Even if one considers Wieland's attitude concerning the world and its institutions at this point, his religious "perversion," and his predilection for "controversial" authors, one concludes that the development of his work in the area of the travesty was unthinkable in the Switzerland of Bodmer's domain and under the restraining influence of Julie Bondely. Wieland's lively temperament, his susceptibility to the wit of Lucian, Swift, and Voltaire could not be harmonized permanently with Swiss conservatism.

The years of his service to the municipal office of his home town, Biberach, offered new avenues to the development of the travesty. In 1764 Wieland undertook his "adventure" novel *Der Sieg der Natur über die Schwärmerey, oder Die Abentheuer des Don Sylvio von Rosalva: Eine Geschichte*, *worinn Alles Wunderbare natürlich zugeht* (Ulm, 1764). Young Wieland had been introduced to Cervantes' *Don Quixote* under the mentorship of J. W. Baumer in Erfurt, and developed a lifelong affinity to the spirit of the great Spaniard. It is Cervantes' colorful work which served as the model for Wieland's novel. I am not advancing the theory that this work be considered a travesty or even a satirical novel, but I nevertheless want to make brief mention of certain striking parodistic features and elements common to the original and Wieland's version. There is, for example, the principal pair of characters—Don Quixote and Sancho Panza in the Spanish source, Don Sylvio and Pedrillo in the work of Wieland. The latter brilliantly parallels the color and personality of the two famous models, translated into the spirit of another age. There is apparently no intention on Wieland's part to take to task Cervantes, or various French fairy tales, or Lucian whose influence is also felt. Wieland's didactic purpose is clear: to cure the hero from his serious case of chronic *Schwärmerei*, also the "disease" of Don Quixote, and to help him regain a sense of reality. In his work, the poet achieves the actual "Sieg der Natur über die Schwärmerei" through the love of the leading heroine, Donna Felicia, as well as by the impact of a fairy tale *Die Geschichte des Prinzen Biribinker* (Part II, Book 6, Chapters 1 and 2). This fairy tale within the novel is original with Wieland, except for some exotic names which occur in it and which are traceable to other sources. It is a *Rahmenerzählung*, narrated by Don Gabriel, a friend of Sylvio. In his tale, Don Gabriel makes a point of carrying his ridicule of the entire fairy enterprise *ad absurdum*, just as the Spanish model had taken to task books of chivalry. But Wieland's scorn extends beyond the realm of an exaggerated fairy world which disowns reality; rather, he employs the fairy tale and its paraphernalia as a vehicle of illustrating questionable pedagogic practices of the time in which vicarious adventures were calculated to stimulate the imagination, and made to suffice in favor of nurturing a wholesome sense of reality through reason and actual experience. Indeed, the most ludicrous figure in the novel is Donna Mencia, Sylvio's aunt and tutor—an undesirable "educator" whose teaching harms her young charge more than it benefits him. Only Sylvio's removal from the radius of her influence, and the "normalcy" of another's well-adjusted views bring about his cure. In the charming, good-naturedly satirical spirit we perceive an early manifestation of Wieland's humorous didacticism—still in prose—which he managed to refine in works to come. Moreover, the title of the novel, and the influence of the two persons chiefly responsible for its hero's cure, are reminiscent of a phase in Wieland's own life in which, through the experience with Sophie La Roche and Count Stadion, he freed himself from the excesses of his own *Schwärmerei*.

Wieland's literary products of the years from 1761 to 1765, probably the period of his most intimate ties with the circle of Warthausen, reflect the taste of his exalted benefactor, Count Stadion, an enlightened statesman, cosmopolite and patron of an elaborate Rococo court. The poet's social rôle at Warthausen, the influence of a prominent "maecenas" and of the French Rococo, but perhaps the impact of his Shakespeare translation, accomplished his ultimate emergence from the "Seraphic" and Pietistic stages of his earlier career. Few works attest to his personal metamorphosis and his eagerness to conform to his patron's wishes more eloquently than the widely criticized *Komische Erzählungen* of 1765 (*cf.* Chapter IV), which, chiefly because of his reliance upon Lucianus Samosatensis for a plot, may probably count as his first genuine travesty.

From the playful, frivolous Rococo atmosphere emerged two fantastic verse epics, *Idris* (1767), later renamed *Idris und Zenide*, and *Der neue Amadis* (1771), both culmination and farewell to Wieland's pure Rococo verse production. In the case of the epyllion, the miniature epic of this period, Wieland's choice of format in itself may be viewed as a parodistic reaction to the static, traditional epic (*cf.* Chapter II). As in *Die Abenteuer des Don Sylvio von Rosalva*, he satirizes an entire literary genre, and the foibles and shortcomings of contemporary society or institutions in the guise of chivalric and fantastic costume, rather than evolving a conscious travesty of the work which served as his model. To be sure, he adapted their prose to verse narratives of considerable finesse. In the five cantos of *Idris*, Wieland fused a multitude of influences and trends from a number of sources, among them Count Anthony Hamilton's prose work *Les Quatre Facardins* which in itself parodies French Rococo literature. Wieland, who greatly admired Hamilton's *esprit*, ambitiously endeavored to make his *Idris* the German counterpart to the work of Hamilton, and possibly even to outdo him by extravagance (VIII, 9). Wieland defended a measure of his individuality and, indeed, his poetic capabilities:

> Was wird der ernsthafte, philosophische, theologische, ökonomische und politische Geist unserer Nation zu einem Werke sagen, das in der ganzen poetischen Welt an Extravaganz seines gleichen weder hat, noch hoffentlich jemals bekommen wird. Stellen Sie sich eine Fabel im Geschmacke der *quatre Facardins* oder des *Bêlier* von Hamilton vor—aber eine Fabel, die keiner andern gleich sieht, die noch aus einem gesunden Kopfe gekommen ist— die Quintessenz aller Abentheuer der Amadise und Feenmährchen.—Und in diesem Plane, unter dieser frivolen Aussenseite Metaphysik, Moral, Entwickelung der geheimsten Federn des menschlichen Herzens, Kritik, Satyre, Charaktere, Gemählde, Leidenschaften, Reflexionen, Sentiments—kurz alles, was Sie wollen, mit Zaubereyen, Geister-Historien, Zweykämpfen, Centauren, Hydern, Gorgonen und Amphibäuen, so schön abgesetzt und durcheinander geworfen, und das alles in einem so mannigfaltigen Styl, so leicht gemahlt, so leicht versifiziert, so tändelhaft gereimt, und das in *ottave rime* (Letter to Geßner, dated July 21, 1766. *DB*, I, 34).

His capricious effervescence is balanced by the elevated and, to be sure, incongruous meter reminiscent of Ariosto's ottava rima—Wieland's first experiment in this difficult discipline, according to Gruber (VIII, 5). The complexity of the characters, ideas, situations, and motifs aims at confusing and delighting the reader. An attempt at comparing the perplexing details with his models would, indeed, be idle. By blending frivolity with morals, fantastic elements with social satire and criticism through a profusion of illustrations, Wieland evolved his coated didactic message: the triumph of the middle-of-the-road approach between two extremists—the Platonist (Idris), and the Hedonist (Itifall)—both in pursuit of the same object, Zenide. An "ideal" couple, Zerbino and Lila, examplifies the sense of moderation. In similar spirit, he elicits common sense—another expression of balance. Wieland's scorn is directed against fools (*cf. Schwärmerei* in *Don Sylvio*) and heroes alike, and suggests his ironic appraisal of each of these dubious categories who, more than any other, it seems, are subject to whims of chance and their own weakness (Sengle, *Arbeiten*, p. 58). At the same time he takes to task the universal evil of complacency:

> Der Erdkreis wäre bald an Narr'n und Helden leer,
> Wenn wir zur Führerin die Logik nehmen müßten.
> . . . . .
> Erfahrung und Vernunft wird nur nicht angehört;
> Wir nennen falsch, was uns in süßem Irrthum stört
> (Canto V, 99, VIII, 220).

The fragmentary nature of the work in itself is a factor of Wieland's irony. The veiled quest for balance is further obscured by a language replete with Rococo apparatus; sumptuous similes, sentimental oxymora, and allegory involving nature add to the veritable cult of the senses which Wieland entertains in this work. Yet, a saucy crispness prevails to the close of the narrative which, like its model, remained fragmentary. In the manner of Lawrence Sterne, Wieland involves the reader as he leaves the conclusion up to his audience:

> Den weisen Leuten, welche nie,
> Wie unserm Helden war, erfuhren,
> . . . . .

> Klingt nichts so schal, als die Figuren
> Verliebter Schwärmerei. Gut, ich verschone sie:
> Der Pinsel fällt mir willig aus den Händen;
> Wer Lust hat mag das Bild und—dieses Werk vollenden!
> (Canto V, 119, VIII, 228).

Similarly, *Der neue Amadis* (1771), a work representative of the decline of German Rococo, can hardly be called a pure travesty. Yet, as in *Idris und Zenide*, there are symptoms which point to the further refinement in Wieland's development into a conscious craftsman of the travesty. If in the eighteen cantos of *Der neue Amadis*, too, Wieland intended a takeoff on the grand epic, the title is surely the only actual link to either of his two possible models, Bernardo Tasso's *Amadigi*, and García Ordóñez de Montalvo's old chivalric narrative *Amadis de Gaula* (XIV, viii). Certainly, one notes a parody on chivalrous society as Wieland portrays his adventurous knights devoid of the traditional set of chivalrous ideals, and detached from the framework of courtly practices. But the world of the *esprit gaulois* repeatedly served Wieland as a backdrop. Presenting his figures grotesquely out of context is analogous to any other portrayal of sham—character or situation alike. In a letter to Gleim, dated October 2, 1769, Wieland himself claimed originality for the work while hinting at the synthetic nature of its classification: "Es ist ein wahres Original; ein Mittelding zwischen allen andern Gattungen von Epischer Poesie, denn es hat von allen etwas."[2] Of the travesty as such he makes no mention. Nevertheless, the influence of Christopher Anstey's social satire *The New Bath Guide* and Alexander Pope's *The Rape of the Lock* is evident in spite of the baffling abundance of fantastic caprices. The world which Wieland portrays here is an artificial, yet by no means a static one, for in the guise of imaginary knights and princesses he attacks the prudishness and hypocrisy of his own society. To be sure, the spirit of arbitrariness which is characteristic of life itself pervades the poem, and mollifies the severity of Wieland's social critique. The illusion of the entire work dominates the apparently negligible plot and its confusing details. Here, as in *Idris und Zenide*, Wieland demonstrated a skeptical attitude not only toward his fantastic creatures but also his exotic personages whose incongruity with their environment enhances the satire. Chance and folly, of which black Tulpan is a personification, play an even more prominent part here than in *Idris und Zenide*. Deliberately artificial creatures enliven the situation through animated dialogue. Its content and the echo of irony are, naturally, alien to the traditional epic.

Wieland's socio-critical inclination did not cease with the passing of the Rococo, only the manner in which he gave it expression. His personal experiences in public service, his highs and lows in office, in short, his continued exposure to society seasoned him with a dose of pessimism and endowed him with a clearer vision for an increasingly objective appraisal of humanity and its shortcomings. The result was a mellowed, detached, ironical image of the society with which he dealt—the ideal of *Heiterkeit* having evolved through a process of insight and thoughtful resignation. Even the political novel *Der goldne Spiegel oder die Könige von Scheschian* (1772) suggests parodistic traits critical of the absolute monarchy in the genealogy of ludicrous, totally inapt rulers (*cf.* Chapter IV). In his *Geschichte des weisen Danischmend und der drei Kalender* (1775), a document of Wieland's further metamorphosis since 1772, and more a revocation of, rather than a supplement to, *Der goldne Spiegel*, he sharply assailed exploitation on the part of organized government and religion, among other issues (*cf.* Chapter IV).

The peak product of Wieland's socio-critical prose period is indubitably his *Geschichte der Abderiten* (1774/1781), a brilliant contribution to the annals of *Narrenliteratur*, this time in the mask of classical antiquity. Mindful of his critics' anticipation of a vast variety of models from real life, Wieland sarcastically brushed aside all would-be speculations, asserting in the preface to the novel that nature served as his sole authority. A genuine reproduction of ludicruous reality, then, was his aim, that is, not to ridicule but to portray that which is ridiculous. If, by its nature, one may categorize the work among the most brilliant and profound in the tradition of fools' literature, one realizes the poet's growing social pessimism or, perhaps, resignation with which he viewed the status of the professions, the inadequacies of the judicial system, as in "Viertes Buch oder der Prozeß um des Esels Schatten"—a classical satire on the shortcomings of legal procedure and, in general, the impotence of reason anywhere. In spite of the ancient costume which Wieland frequently chose, one can hardly classify the work a travesty. Because of its timelessness and universal validity, Sengle (p. 336) refutes the frequent designation of "satirical novel." In spite of aspects which were long held to be objects of Wieland's satire, such as Biberach and the limited mentality of its citizens—especially of its officials—, and the mayor's widow, Cateau von Hillern, who is immortalized as the influential Frau Salabanda, Wieland maintained tongue-in-cheek that his honest intention was to create a tale—"ein Mährchen"—involving male and female fools of every category but of no definite identity.[3] The *Geschichte der Abderiten* reflects his further detachment, the increasing resignation, and the triumph of humor over mere satire, a quality which distinguishes his *Oberon*.

The somber verse narrative *Geron der Adeliche* (1776) was adapted from the account *Gyron-le-Courtois* from the series *Romans de Chevalerie* in the *Bibliothèque Universelle des Romans*, I (October 1776). A tragic mood prevails in this adaptation which appears to be remarkably free from parodistic intent. By contrast, the other product of the same year, *Gandalin oder Liebe um Liebe*, is an opus in the lighter vein. Its French source is the episode *La Dame Invisible* of Paul Scarron's *Roman Comique* which appeared in the *Bibliothèque Universelle des Romans*, II (January 1776), 118 ff.[4] The basic motif in both the original and Wieland's version is that of disguise and revealed identity for the purpose of testing a lover's fidelity. Wieland's interpretation, and the attitude of the characters in given situations, especially where morals are concerned, constitute the nature of his travesty which once more assumes fantastic guise in a milieu reminiscent of the Round Table. The poet is not intent upon either imitating or distorting the original hero, Don Carlos of Arragon; his Gandalin is less sharply defined. A fairly nondescript knight, one of the youngest, least experienced but most ardent admirers of Fräulein Sonnemon, Gandalin agrees to her condition of testing his professed sentiments: he must dispatch himself on a three year adventure without shunning exposure to amorous temptation. The uncommonly desirable lady is not masked, but has identity (heiress to the Count of Brabant) and the capacity of evoking a grotesquely humorous sense of competition among her overambitious courtiers:

> Die Junkern eiferten, buhlten, stritten,
> Liebten und liebelten, tanzten und ritten
> Rings um die holde Zaubrerin,
> Wie Hummeln um ihre Königin...
> (XXI, 50).

Again, it is a social stratum rather than an individual that receives Wieland's scorn. Absolute steadfastness and fidelity are the virtues to be tested—a theme which later reappears in *Oberon*. The condition stipulates no threat, but rather, promise of

> ...der Minne Lohn...
> Ihr Herz mit allen Zubehören!
> (XXI, 59).

Wherever Wieland enlarges upon his model it is hardly an expansion of the fairly primitive plot, but instead a pseudo-philosophical elaboration or ironical reflection on love, its prominence, its many shades, and a protest against hypocrisy and an all too rigid *Tugend* (*cf*. prologue, which anticipates the hero and the ultimate resolution with good-natured irony). Wieland's rendering outdoes his French model in color and sensuous transport: he dispenses with the mundane intrigue of his source (kidnapping, feigned message, etc.), relying instead on the time-tested backdrop of the "Romantic" setting and on *Feerei*. Gandalin's test of virtue is far more exacting than Carlos' who is forcibly transported to a magnificent mansion where he must withstand—and does—the charms, entreaties and tears of the adorable princess Porcia.

Wieland introduces the element of choice which compounds the intricacy and, of course, heightens the irony. One evening Gandalin encounters "...eine Jungfrau (dem Ansehn nach)..." (XXI, 67) on horseback, beckoning him to follow her to a certain castle where the test of tests commences. The factor of the veiled identity, insignificant as it may seem on the surface, undergoes a subtle change, too. The French source provokes the hero's curiosity by first exposing him to a masked unknown who proceeds to entice him until he is involuntarily confronted with the unveiled beauty of the same identity. Wieland, on the other hand, has his hero fully aware of the identity and social prominence of his adored lady. Yet, he falls victim to another's beckoning. He gives in to the lure of adventure—polite adventure—and he is immediately confronted with peril. The element of risk continues in the person of the veiled unknown languidly posing on a sofa as the caliph's daughter, "Je länger je lieber." She arouses Gandalin's chivalric protective sense by pretending to be under a wicked enchantment: any man who sets eye on her would be bound to go out of his mind. Therefore, she is doomed to be permanently masked until a knight would unconditionally love her without having seen her. Gandalin cheerfully accepts the challenge. In spite of twinges of conscience he becomes thoroughly entranced with the exotic stranger to whose charms he is exposed day after day. At this point, Wieland takes the opportunity to insert a word to moralists and Philistines, one of his favorite objects of criticism:

> Es ist, ich muß es selbst gestehen,
> Abscheulich!—...
> ...sich gleich
> Bei jeder Versuchung von ihren Begierden
> Hinreißen lassen! Moralisirten
> Die Leute nur sieben Minuten lang
> Mit kaltem Blut erst über die Sachen,
> Sie würden solche Streiche nicht machen!

> ...Herr Sittenlehrer,
> So dankt dem Himmel doch dafür
> Daß es so ist! Was wolltet denn Ihr
> Beginnen, ihr andern Weltbekehrer,
> Wenn's anders würde?
> (XXI, 106-107).

The hero's dilemma, of course, is loving two fair ladies. When he admits his predicament to his beloved Sonnemon, and learns that she is identical with his temptress, she is prepared graciously to forgive him. She had exercised the caution not to trust anyone but herself to test him, and refused to consider a man less reliable than he. The French hero passes the test of virtue, so that there is no obstacle in the way for "Ces heureux Amans...de resserer...des nœuds formés par l'amour" (*Bibliothèque*, II, January 1776, 126). Wieland resolved the conflict between passion and fidelity on an ironical note:

> ...Du warst nie ungetreu,
> Und bist es noch nicht, hast mich immer
> Geliebt, und alles ist Feerei...
> (XXI, 152).

The basic difference between the original and Wieland's version lies in the very conflict: while the hero of the French source maintains what Sengle (p. 351) calls "starre, rationale Tugend," Wieland is infinitely more humane and psychologically plausible in his treatment.

The period from 1777 to 1780 is generally regarded as the peak of Wieland's "humorous classicism." Most of the master travesties are indeed products of this period of artistic maturity (*cf*. Chapter IV). In *Oberon* (1780) Wieland's virtuosity excels. Here he eloquently demonstrated his ability to blend a multitude of elements and moods, and to harmonize tragedy, humor, and irony within one voluminous "Gedicht in zwölf Gesängen." With this work the poet's name was, and perhaps still is, synonymous. Its waning popularity during the current century may perhaps be ascribed to the decline which the epic genre on the whole has been experiencing with the rising prevalence of the novel.

Oberon, more than any other of Wieland's works, represents a synthesis of elements from the literature of many divergent worlds. The poet involved French, English, German, and Oriental sources or elements which he wove into a fascinating fairy epic. He satisfied his "Romantic" inclination by dipping into the chivalrous age for the setting of the plot, by calling upon the Oriental world for the exotic touch, and upon the fairy world, indeed, its sovereign, to play the dominant rôle. In the preface addressed *An den Leser*, Wieland names as sources for his plot the old French chivalric epic *Huon de Bordeaux*, an extract of which was known to him through a prose version of the old epic by Count Louis Tressan de la Vergne.[5] He further gives credit to Geoffrey Chaucer's *The Merchant's Tale* from *The Canterbury Tales*, and William Shakespeare's *A Midsummer-Night's Dream* for their conception of Oberon, although only Shakespeare actually used the name of Oberon. The Oberon of the chivalric epic plays the part of a *deus ex machina*, and has little in common with the fairy king of the English sources, nor with Wieland's own image of the fairy king.

Wieland's *Oberon* was enthusiastically accepted, endorsed by great minds, admired and loved by the reading public, and popularized through numerous translations, reviews, lectures, and essays. The work earned Wieland unreserved praise and laurels from Goethe who conceived of it as a sterling masterpiece of poetic art. Might it not appear sacrilegious to attach the stigma of the travesty in the conventional sense to such a renowned poetic *tour de force*? As has been pointed out in the Introduction to this study, anything can indeed be travestied, and Wieland possessed the unique ability to ameliorate his sources by adding humor, dimension, color—in short, to endow his creations with the quality of humanity. In his *Oberon*, perhaps more than in any other work, one is aware of the special blend of "sweet travesty," a rendering which aesthetically enhances his model rather than seeking to depreciate its niveau by pejorative means. To be sure, certain portions of the work are entirely free from scorn and even moving in their sentiment, especially the idyllic island episode, Wieland's most prominent original contribution to the *Oberon* epic (*cf.* Madame de Staël's work *De l'Allemagne*, in which she lauds Wieland's pure sentiment in presenting a spirit of contentedness, tranquility, and modest domestic joys in the middle of a barren, inhospitable island.[6])

Wieland's main plot source, *Huon de Bordeaux* in Tressan's drab prose version, is encumbered with unnecessary repetitions, subplots, and side-issues. Again, we see Wieland's successful efforts in streamlining the narration while elevating the diction. In contrast with the somewhat pedantic, unimaginative prose of his model, the varying rhythm of his eight-line stanza, and his generous rhetorical devices (metaphors, interjections, colorful descriptions), lend immediacy and anticipate the multiplicity of themes issuing from the worlds of the "marvelous," of Christian knighthood, and of the Pagan Orient. The following passages from the model and from Wieland's adaptation, respectively, will serve to illustrate the contrast: "Il [Gérasme] le conduit... jusques sur les bords de la mer rouge,... & le fait passer en Arabie. A peine y étoient, ils entrés, que le Chef d'une horde d'Arabes vagabonds vient les attaquer.... Cette aventure & plusieurs autres, inutiles à rapporter, ayant à peine retardé de quelques heures la marche d'Huon..." (*Bibliothèque*, II, April 1778, 30-31). Hüon's successful encounter with a troop of Arabs has not only grim battlefield scenes; Wieland also interjects a brief idealization of peaceful country life:

> Wie selig, denkt er, wär's, in diesen Hütten wohnen!
> Vergeblicher Wunsch! Ihn ruft sein Schicksal anderwärts (Canto II, 9, XXIII, 53).

As he and Scherasmin, his travel companion, continue their journey the poet heightens the suspense in polished metaphorical language, which adds to the mysterious atmosphere:

> Ein unbekanntes Was, das ihn wie ein Magnet

> Nach Bagdad zieht, scheint allen seinen Blicken
> Die scharfe Spitze abzuknicken
> Und macht, daß jeder Reiz an ihm verloren geht
> (Canto III, 43, XXIII, 97).

The French source, of course, yields the name of Wieland's hero, Hüon, whose biography is told in his adventures, and whose name constitutes the title of the prose narrative. Wieland's Hüon is also the protagonist of the poem which is, however, named after the fairy character, the dwarf, by whose interference the action develops. This shift in emphasis from the chivalrous central figure to a legendary creature is a subtle device of superimposing the fantastic element upon a member of human society, thus allowing for greater freedom of movement in plot development and conclusion. At the same time, the subordination of the knight deals a blow to the venerated ideals of chivalry and perhaps seeks to rock the established immunities of the aristocratic "caste." Wieland's Oberon is by no means a mere *deus ex machina*. By virtue of his powers, the elfin king assumes the function of a supreme being, styled at once fate and providence. One perceives Oberon, rather than Christianity, and much less, religion, as Hüon's emotional mainstay. Rather than depending on the tenets of his faith and its comfort, Hüon acts, derives strength and secures aid from Oberon. With Oberon's help, instead of by trickery which is often employed in the Tressan source, he overcomes the most incredible obstacles, perseveres, and finally succeeds in fulfilling his fantastic mission. His guide—perhaps his conscience—Oberon is as much the benevolent father image (*cf.* Canto V, where he blesses the love of Hüon and Rezia), as the stern legislator (*cf.* Canto VI, in which he pronounces his commandment banning physical love for the leading characters). He is the offended authority endowed with the powers to punish instantly and thoroughly (*cf.* Canto VII, where the lovers prove to have ignored his command), and finally, the conciliatory spirit (*cf.* Canto XII, where, after a myriad of trials, the lovers have persevered in the face of extreme perils). Presumably, Wieland intended his Oberon to represent the didactic element without, however, seeming to be a moralizing authoritarian. His wrath underscored by thunder, Oberon truly appears as a nature spirit who is able to incite a terrible tempest on the sea which nearly annihilates the lovers for having broken their vow. The degree to which Wieland mirrors the rôle and the "romantic" conception of nature sets him apart from his precursors and lends animation uncommon to the world of the travesty.

Max Koch in his monograph *Das Quellenverhältniß von Wielands Oberon* submits that Wieland's main original contribution lies probably in the "recasting" of the character of Oberon: "... das koboldartige mußte verschwinden, während das menschliche in Oberon verstärkt wurde...."[7] Moreover, Koch hints at the presence of the element of salvation which, to be sure, is evident also in the French model. He contrasts the characters of the two versions: "Aber so wenig anziehend Oberon bei Tressan erscheint, so fand Wieland doch schon hier für seinen geisterkönig das motiv einer 'erlösungsbedürftigkeit' vor, welches der haupthebel seiner eigenen dichtung zu werden bestimmt war" (Koch, p. 4). Oberon, the fantastic character, seeks salvation through eventual reconciliation with Titania. By reconciling the emperor, Hüon, the mortal, endeavors his own rehabilitation, that is, "salvation" here on earth. The concern for redemption does not seem to extend beyond the realm of mundane matters. Basically, it involves extrication from the intricately difficult situation in which Hüon, initially a guiltless character, finds himself. The adventures, however colorful and daring, are undertaken in an effort of righteous self-vindication. Oberon, guardian to Hüon, is aware of the latter's fundamental purity and immunity from any enchantment, while those stained with vice are vulnerable to his powers. Although his French counterpart, the *Roi de Féerie*, also manifests a kindly disposition toward the hero himself, Wieland's modification elevates Oberon above the generally prankish leaning of the model. Wieland is obviously more concerned with Oberon's impact than with his appearance and background. He makes no attempt at distorting his physical features, and even ignores Tressan's account of his fantastic history: the son of Julius Caesar and of the fairy Gloriande, Oberon upon the curse of a vicious aunt had been stunted in growth at the age of four. To Wieland, Oberon is "Ein Knäbchen, schön, wie .../Der Liebesgott..." (Canto II, 28, XXIII, 61)—an epithet hardly consonant with the stature of an omnipotent being, but sure to produce the desired humorous imbalance.

Wieland parallels many situations already present in his model. Neither version is complimentary in its treatment of the most exalted nobles. The intrigues of Charlemagne's villainous son, Charlot, his falsehood, and finally his attempts upon Hüon's life, are scarcely becoming the house of the Holy Roman Empire. On the other hand, one is afforded a glimpse at chivalric precepts when Hüon—alleged killer of Charlot—emerges victorious from single combat with his accuser. In contrast, one observes the emperor's skepticism on the outcome of the ordeal: he is inclined to "pardon" Hüon on condition of fulfilling an absurdly complex assignment which almost amounts to a death sentence and represents a bizarre distortion of chivalric deeds of valor. Having traversed an enchanted forest, successfully overcome a giant, withstood the perils of a pagan court, a shipwreck, life on a desert island, pirates, superhuman temptation, having even faced death at the stake, one sees Hüon engaged in yet another quite realistic chivalrous tournament (Canto XII). Curiously, the appearance of Oberon, a pretty, puerile god, had caused Hüon and his traveling companion to take to their heels (Canto II). Thus, some genuine chivalric aspects are mingled with fantastic paraphernalia and comic touches which, to be sure, manage to cast doubt on the entire chivalric institution.

Having passed through the "purgatory" of the *Sturm und Drang*, Wieland shows a vestigial tendency toward Germanizing the original French names (*e.g.*, Amaury de Hautefeuille becomes Amory von Hohenblat, Girard is Gerard, Thiéry d'Ardennes is Dietrich von Ardenne). In general, he seems to strive for increased popularity (*Volkstümlichkeit*): Thus, the emperor Charlemagne becomes simply *der Kaiser* or just Karl. The figure of Scherasmin, senior companion to Hüon, is modeled after Gérasme of the Tressan source so far as his name and some of his courtly virtues, such as bravery and unselfish, loyal devotion to his liege lord are concerned. The motif of fear and avoidance of Oberon is likewise borrowed from the French source. Yet, Wieland's humor—his additive—works a significant change in Hüon's personality. The poet's modification of Tressan's stereotype knight appears here not as a burlesque contrast character but as an intrinsically human mentor figure. In evaluating the relationship between Hüon and Scherasmin, Koch (pp. 24-25) points out a vague resemblance of that "duo" with Cervantes' famous pair in *Don Quixote;* of course, it also recalls Wieland's parallel of Don Sylvio and Pedrillo. The sultan's daughter, Tressan's Esclarmonde, becomes animated through Wieland's gentle metamorphosis. Her development from princess to devoted wife and loving mother, through adversity to final triumph, lends her figure dimension and credibility. The change of the heroine's name which marks prominent segments of her biography also indicates a change in milieu. In order to create a counterpart to the chivalric pair, Wieland conceived the character of Fatme, Rezia's maid and confidante. The rôle of the socially subordinate companion is reminiscent of theatrical tradition. Canto XII with its intrigue, calculated misconceptions, and the turmoil over mistaken identities certainly has its share of stage appeal.

Although all of Wieland's borrowed characters undergo some degree of transformation, there is little evidence of malicious distortion, save perhaps the figure of the Sultan, the only one who suffers at Wieland's hands. Here and elsewhere (*cf. Das Wintermährchen, Schach Lolo*, or in the genealogy of sultans in the *Geschichte des weisen Danischmend und der drei Kalender*), his negative portrayal of Oriental potentates—possibly his best characterization—reflects a living protest against the excesses of courtly life, and the inadequacies in government anywhere. Wieland seems to delight in reducing his sultans to caricatures —probably the only stratum of society to receive consistently this devastatingly berating treatment. The grotesquely humorous sultan, Rezia's father, is simply "der Kalif" to

Wieland, while his French source accords him title, name, and some desirable traits of character as Amiral Gaudisse.

The milieu of the pagan court prompts Wieland's critique of hypocrisy no less than the area of the church. Indeed, both are repeatedly shown to be the object of his censure (*cf. Sixt und Clärchen, Die Wasserkufe, Schach Lolo*). He parallels his model in the theme of detecting hypocrisy by means of Oberon's magic horn. In Canto II he causes a procession of monks and nuns to succumb to a violent fit of dancing elicited by the soft sounds of the horn. He makes the point that only "pure" Hüon remains immune. Identical effects occur in Canto V where the horn serves to expose a vice-ridden court, with the exception of virtuous Rezia. In either incident, the fantastic device tends to mitigate Wieland's pointed criticism.

The theme of the sultan's conversion—his conversion to Christianity is one of the conditions imposed by Charlemagne— is varied by Wieland. While the *amiral* staunchly refuses to renounce his own faith and is struck dead on the spot by an invisible hand, acceptance of Christianity by the obviously notorious, morally depraved *Kalif* becomes a matter of compromise—the less painful evil, so to speak—in place of forfitting beard and teeth, another token of submission. The motif of conversion reoccurs in both versions. Here and in related issues involving precepts of the church, Wieland gently weaves the fabric of his subtle travesty. His delicate irony prevents virulence and guards the civility of his tone. Fair Esclarmonde of Tressan's version is instructed in the teachings of Christianity by Hüon whom she visits in the dungeon and eventually frees from imprisonment. Oberon advises the hero to take her to Rome and there to make her his lawful wife with the blessings of the church. After a perplexing myriad of adventures and adversities, Tressan's couple does obtain papal absolution and a church wedding in Rome before returning to France. Wieland does not ignore the influence of the church, but her functions in his work are marginal and conventional by nature: in Canto I one learns that Hüon left Rome with the Pope's, his uncle's, blessings for his undertaking, and paid a visit to the Holy Sepulchre as a condition for success. However, the poet happily resolves his fairy epic without the benefit of papal absolution or church-sanctioned wedding. Instead, he shifts the absolution motif onto Oberon who, ultimately appeased by the lovers' fidelity almost unto death at the stake, miraculously rescues them from further adversity and doom. Indeed, the compound source of the hero's felicity at the conclusion of the poem is mundane in nature. Having reconciled the emperor by presenting to him all the tangible signs of his atonement, Hüon is at last exonerated and fully rehabilitated. He then is rejoicing in his fortuitous homecoming with his family, and in his regained status. His is not the image of the itinerant knight returning from a crusade of adventures *ad maiorem dei gloriam*, for in spite of the color and high spirit, one perceives not so much a manifestation of chivalrous glory or Christian beatitude as a thoroughly human feeling of relief. Wieland's conception of chivalry in *Oberon*, Richard Newald holds, is not one of "...weltliches und geistiges Rittertum oder Heldentum des Glaubens, sondern menschliche Bewährung in der Gefahr. Doch steht diese Bewährung nicht unter dem starren, unverletzbaren Gesetz des Stoizismus, der Bezwingung der Leidenschaften, sondern unter dem milderen, verstehenden Gesetz der Liebe und deren läuternder Macht."[8] The promise of future happiness—presumably earthly—is, of course, in keeping with the fairy atmosphere which traditionally suggests a spirit of continuity, even beyond the happy end.

Wieland's characteristic secularism colors the development of the relationship between Hüon and Rezia. His champion Oberon—not loyalty to the dictates of the Decalogue—imposes the abstinence requirement upon the two lovers. While retaining this motif from his model, the narrator, through Oberon, anticipates the inevitable in a tone reflecting skepticism and resignation stemming from his intimate knowledge of human nature. Oberon's only threat is that in case the lovers break their promise, he would have to become separated from them forever:

> Er sagt's, und seufzt, und stiller Kummer schwillt
> In seinem Aug'...
> (Canto VI, 10, XXIII, 191).

Wieland's Hüon, too, instructs Rezia in the teachings of Christianity, a faith which she embraces eagerly. She is baptized by a member of the clergy who happens to be aboard ship, and assumes the name Amanda. Again, Wieland deviates from the spirit of his French model by underscoring the sensuous element without being insensitive to the fine nuances of tender communication between the lovers. Their constant togetherness on shipboard, far more than Rezia's conversion, heightens their mutual attraction. Wieland capitalizes on the erotic element in colorful metaphors:

> Er fühlt die süße Gefahr. O, soll es möglich seyn,
> Du Schönste, ruft er oft, bis Rom es auszuhalten,
> So wickle dich in sieben Schleier ein!
> Verstecke jeden Reiz in tausend kleine Falten;
> Laß über dieses Arms lebend'ges Elfenbein
> Die weiten Aermel bis zur Fingerspitze fallen,
> Und ach! Freund Oberon, vor allen
> Verwandle bis dahin mein Herz in kalten Stein!
> (Canto VI, 21, XXIII, 195).

His lines in Canto XII recall a variation of the theme involving tested virtue of which he repeatedly makes a humorously conscientious issue in order to illustrate convincingly the trials to which especially the male is exposed:

> Er kämpft den schwersten Kampf, den je seit Josefs Zeit
> Ein Mann gekämpft, den edlen Kampf der Tugend
> Und Liebestreu' und feuervollen Jugend
> Mit Schönheit, Reiz und heißer Ueppigkeit
> (Canto XII, 19, XXIV, 101).

Virtue, one of the chief concerns and bywords of the literary Enlightenment, suggested to Wieland not so much a fixed standard on the moral scale but rather an issue of all too human wavering (*cf.* Chapter IV). This apparently frivolous surface trifling with the lofty ideal of virtue brings him into sharp focus as an accomplished master of the travesty in an age when few reputable *literati* dared risk public censure for discoloring the well-defined concept. In dealing with the abstraction of *Tugend*, Wieland called on the quality of the intangible to guard his tirades against sinking to the niveau of the farce. To this end, he succeeded remarkably with the device of the rhetorical question:

> Allein, wie lange wird er ihrem süßen Flehn,
> Den Küssen voller Gluth, dem zärtlich wilden Drücken
> An ihren Busen, widerstehn?
> (Canto XII, 19, XXIV, 101).

Or, he simply employed the fleeting epithet of the *je ne sais quoi* culture which lends sufficient propriety to a measure of suggestiveness, in one word—interest. By invoking the elusive "Ich weiß nicht was," the poet manages to be alternately or simultaneously mysterious, discreet, tactful, and provocative (cf. the previously quoted passage from Canto III, pp. 47-48).

Neither *Tugendseligkeit* nor base eroticism has a place in Wieland's work. The varied motif of the test is repeatedly employed as an agent for tempering the emotions. Aside from the superhuman, totally fantastic mission which Hüon undertakes on his own behalf, he and Rezia are subjected to many a trial—moral and physical. In spite of their noble birth and genteel disposition, the young, immature lovers fail the first test, that is, they fall victim to human frailty, and are obliged to atone for "Der Liebe süßes Gift" (Canto VII, 11, XXIII, 238). During a probationary period which is fraught with anxiety and privation they become seasoned to withstand calamity, toil, and temptation. By submitting to discipline, they learn to derive strength from each other, and eventually *earn* conjugal happiness. Adversity is not rarely a preceptress in the process of maturation and purgation. Being subjected to the second test, Hüon and Rezia conquer Oberon's previous skepticism and emerge victorious; as Sengle observes, "Den Gereiften und Geläuterten gelingt, woran die Unerfahrenen scheitern mußten" (Sengle, *Arbeiten*, p. 67). Wieland's intensification of the human element and the natural plot development extend also to events involving supernatural characters.

In Canto VII he retarded the action by interspersing the episode of *January and May*, according to combined source elements mainly from Chaucer, Pope, and Shakespaere. The frame of the tale is provided by Scherasmin who seeks to divert the lovers' attention:

> Zuletzt schlägt er, da alle Mittel fehlen,
> Zur Abendkürzung vor, ein Mährchen zu erzählen.
> Ein Mährchen nennt' er es, wiewohl es freilich
> mehr
> Als Mährchen war
> (Canto VI, 34-35, XXIII, 200-201).

Wieland's English models, themselves masterpieces of sharply satirical wit in verse, leave him little room to enlarge upon the parody. In the adaptation of this episode, too, the quintessence of Wieland's achievement resides in the "how" rather than in the "what."

The narration of the episode, intended as a pleasant pastime, carries a definite, didactic purpose. Literature is replete with the theme involving marriage of young, attractive women to socially, economically—but not physically—superior men who are considerably their seniors. The contrast between partners of such an incongruous match, and many a problem resulting from the imbalance, have repeatedly been the object of satirical wit—with or without didactic intention on the part of the author. It is hardly astonishing that Wieland was attracted by the popular motif of questionable wedded bliss and the likelihood of its universal appeal because it lends itself to derision on all levels of sophistication.

While Chaucer's version represents a *Rahmenerzählung* with a prologue and an epilogue, narrated by the Merchant, Pope's adaptation, entitled *January and May*, shows tendencies of independence of its context in *The Canterbury Tales*. It was written circa 1704, and published in 1709. Koch (p. 54) concludes that Wieland followed mainly Pope's version, but also had reference to the Tyrwhitt edition (1775-1778) of Chaucer's works. Indeed, the evidence tends to point predominantly to the Pope model.

Although there is a striking resemblance in plot elements, characters, spirit, and iambic meter, each successive rendering of the episode becomes more compact; naturally, the existing differences among the three versions encompass far more than those of format. On the surface, each rendering is but a paraphrase of a previously existing one. Yet, in the thoughtful modulation and adaptation of the plot to prevailing conventions of propriety, each poet achieves remarkable quality in his own right. Each succeeds in harmonizing a wholesome attitude toward the institution of marriage while satirizing the characters involved, essentially to a didactic end.

Wieland follows Chaucer and Pope in the plot elements. A sixty-five year old lecher marries a sixteen year old who soon finds comfort in the old man's squire. In Wieland's rendering certain innovations concerning the characters occur—variations in names and some attitudes, as well as the introduction of the Oberon-Titania subplot which is relatively superficially treated by Chaucer and Pope. Wieland is far less elaborate than his models in the exposition. He departs from the tradition of his sources by altering the names of his characters, as indicated. His version of January is Gangolf whose name carries no special significance, yet it imparts a ludicrous quality. It is interesting to note that Wieland's only reference to this original name comes in a simile on the appraisal of the wedded pair whose partners resemble one another like January and May (Canto VI, 42, XXIII, 204). The "worthy knight" of the English sources becomes simply an "Edelmann," a vaguer and less period-bound, hence more universally stereotype nobleman. The poet cleverly contrasts the aristocrat's mentality with his chronological age by employing a play on color:

> ...an Weisheit ziemlich grün,
> Wiewohl sehr grau an Bart und Haaren;
> (Canto VI, 36, XXIII, 201).

Wieland was not given to bowdlerizing—an attitude ascribed to the influence of the *Sturm und Drang*—as he condemns his hero's past:

> Dem war, nachdem er lang' sein sündliches
> Vergnügen
> Daran gehabt,...
> Herum zu ziehn, und, wo er Eingang fand,
> Bei seines Nächsten Weib zu liegen;
> Ihm, sag' ich, war zuletzt der Einfall aufgestiegen,
> Den steifen Hals, noch an des Lebens Rand
> Ins sanfte Joch der heil'gen Eh' zu schmiegen
> (Canto VI, 37, XXIII, 201-202).

Despite his uninhibited condemnation of the old man's promiscuous conduct, Wieland is less revealing in his criticism of Gangolf's state of perversion and self-centeredness. He also devotes fewer lines to the elaboration on any material or moral speculations, but turns immediately and with great care to the selection of the spouse, fair Rosette, the May of his version:

> Mit viel Geschmack und wohl verkühltem Blut
> Sucht er ein Kind sich aus, wie er's zu Tisch und
> Bette,
> Zu Scherz und Ernst, gerade nöthig hätte,
> Zumal zur Sicherheit; ein Mädchen, fromm und gut,
> Unschuldig, sittsam, unerfahren,
> Keusch wie der Mond und frei von aller eiteln Lust,
> Jung überdieß, pechschwarz von Aug' und Haaren,
> Von Farbe rosenhaft, und rund von Arm und Brust
> (Canto VI, 38, XXIII, 202).

Wieland's squire, Walter, appears less culpable than his scheming, thoroughly contemptible counterparts of the

English versions. In spite of the perfidy of the design, Rosette, too, is less reprehensible:

...Rosette war ein Kind,
...war froh und leicht gesinnt,
Und sah in ihrem künftigen Herrn und Gatten
Nichts als den Mann, der sie zur großen Dame
                macht,
Ihr reiche Kleider gab und tausend schöne Sachen,
Die Kindern, wie sie war, bei Tage Kurzweil
                machen;
An andres hatte noch ihr Herzchen nie gedacht
                (Canto VI, 41, XXIII, 203).

The subplot, the controversy between the fairy king and queen (Pluto and Prosperina to Chaucer; "pigmy-king" and "little fairy-queen" to Pope), is less broadly treated in the English sources, and basically involves the moral shortcomings of the female. The garden where the fairy plot develops is the scene of the young wife's shameful indiscretion with the handsome squire in the presence of her blind husband, an incident which, more than any other, evokes a feeling mixed of pity and contempt for the old man. Wieland parallels his models in manifesting a more rigid conception of guilt and punishment of crime on the part of the fairy king, versus a more relenting attitude of the queen. To be sure, Wieland's royal fairy couple, Oberon and Titania—obviously borrowed from Shakespeare's *A Midsummer-Night's Dream*—is not introduced into the text until the moment Rosette is climbing the pear tree, as if momentarily to divert the reader's attention from her impending indiscretion. The original, farcical elements of the scence are retained without extraneous distortion: the wife's exposure through Oberon upon the old man's miraculous recovery from his optical malfunction, her clever extrication attempts through the grace of Titania, the husband's rage of frenzy at beholding the scene, and finally the humoring, conciliatory efforts. In the resolution of the feud, Wieland's Rosette reflects a distinct quality of *Empfind-*

samkeit—another ironical touch when viewed in the light of the *Tugendseligkeit* of his age. Her sensitive remonstrance to Gangolf's harshness, "...mit solchen harten Reden/Dein treues Weib zu morden...." (Canto VI, 95, XXIII, 226) has no parallel in either of the earlier versions. In the scene of the couple's ultimate reconciliation which concludes the episode in both English versions, the German poet capitalizes on Rosette's tearfulness, doleful eyes, and heaving bosom, thereby underscoring the emotionality.

Wieland is independent in his treatment of the conclusion. He feels compelled somehow to dispose of the fairy couple whom Chaucer and Pope have left several stanzas ago. Oberon conceives of Rosette's vindication as a triumph of Titania, the benefactress of deceitful womankind. He cedes victory to her but not without making a partisan issue of it, and in a tone of bitter irony thanks her for enlightening him as to the real state of her loyalty. In five successive stanzas he elaborates on his solemn oath to leave Titania and to remain separated from her until he encounters a pair of unconditionally faithful lovers. Unmoved by Titania's pleas and his own remorse, Oberon is steadfast in his vow, and—so the narrator reminds us—has not shown himself to mankind since; instead, he is out to disturb and torment lovers after the fashion of a malicious goblin. Not until the appearance of Hüon and Rezia, indeed a pair of perfect lovers, does Oberon have occasion for a reunion with Titania. Wieland's personal sentiment is reflected in Oberon's attitude, as Sengle (p. 365) observes: "Indem er [Oberon] schwört, sich nur dann wieder mit Titania zu versöhnen, wenn er ein treues Menschenpaar findet, stellt er die Frage nach dem Wesen des Menschen. Er erwartet nicht, daß viele gut und edel seien; die Torheit und Bosheit der Majorität ist ein Gesetz der Welt... er sucht den edlen Menschen. Er wird zunächst enttäuscht. Wieland kehrt nicht einfach zur alten Vorbilddichtung zurück." Wieland achieved continuity of the interspersed *Rahmenerzählung* and the main plot while lending the episode a fairy tale character, despite its otherwise naturalistic impact.

Again, one sees no attempt at investing any of the existing

characters with bodily grotesqueness—their mental and moral makeup, as well as their respective situations, are sufficiently bizarre. Here again, Wieland employed character shortcomings, sex, even beauty, as intended instruments of moral correction. Pope's, but more so, Chaucer's measure of bawdiness is considerably diluted; yet, in the spirited passages the reader perceives insolence next to elegance in good balance. Wieland's lyrical, euphonious touch tends to mellow the crassness of the subject.

While Wieland conveys the same message as his models—only more concisely—his aesthetic refinement serves to half-veil the realism of the situation. Koch (p. 52) actually credits him with ennobling the "old lascivious farce" (*Schwank*) by means of the introduction of the Oberon-Titania subplot which he hails as a unique artistic device. In *Oberon*, Wieland's ability to create moods reaches its peak and manages to de-emphasize the didactic and the parodistic content alike.

Subsequent narratives which Wieland adapted from more extensive prose sources lack the color and lure of his imaginative style. The witty *piquanterie* of earlier years gives way to more empirical topics and a static expression which is generally ascribed to the poet's advancing years and increasing disillusionment. An uninspired tone pervades his *Das Hexameron von Rosenhain* (published 1805). The sober mood reflects the dual motivation for this work: the need for material and emotional recuperation after the death of his wife. Title and prose are modeled after Giovanni Boccaccio's *Decameron*, while the work bears some resemblance to Goethe's *Unterhaltungen deutscher Ausgewanderten* (1794-1795). In spite of the sobriety, Wieland could not resist a jibe at hypocrisy. In the *Vorbericht* he has the narrator impose the condition that all so-called "empfindsame Familiengeschichten," and "moral" tales, "worin lauter in Personen verwandelte Tugenden und Laster, lauter Menschen aus der Unschuldswelt, lauter Ideale von Güte, Edelmuth, Selbstverläugnung und grenzenloser Wohlthätigkeit, aufgeführt werden, ein für alle Mal ausgeschlossen seyn sollten" (XXIX, vii). Nevertheless, such elements pervade some of the narrative. In the tale entitled *Die*

Entzauberung, featuring probably the last occurrence of fairies in Wieland's work, these mythical creatures are instrumental in obtaining a title of nobility, money, and a bride for the deserving hero: "Wir Feen...sind, wie bekannt, sonst keine Freundinnen von Mißheirathen, und sorgen immer dafür, daß die Königstöchter, die sich in Hirtenknaben, oder die Prinzen, die sich in Gänsemädchen und Aschenbrödel verlieben, am Ende ihresgleichen in ihnen finden" (XXIX, 112).

In this chapter I have shown Wieland's early parodistic talent, as well as its relatively slow and erratic development. None of the works discussed in this chapter is free from elements of the travesty; on the other hand, few can justifiably be termed pure travesties. In the recasting of his long epic sources—mostly into verse narratives of a high artistic niveau—Wieland's inevitable tendency toward minimization not only in volume but also in the intensity of the emotions involved can be seen. Judging from the succinct quality of his products, it would appear that he indeed preferred the shorter, less conspicuous literary genres, even for models from which to fashion his travesties *en miniature*. The font of the more compact narratives (especially of antique derivation), the fairy tale, the legend, and the fable, yielded the metal for his most unique and truly pure travesties which earned him the reputation as a master craftsman of this somewhat problematic genre.

CHAPTER IV

THE LESSER GENRES

1

THE SHORT MIXED NARRATIVE

As pointed out in Chapter III, the evolution of Wieland's travesty was a slow process. Neither the very young, immature nor the aging poet possessed the subtle touch necessary for creating highly artistic products in this genre. Indeed, his master travesties coincide with the peak period of his literary career. This observation may be made regardless of the nature of source material. Quantity as well as quality of his travesties or dominant elements thereof are directly proportionate to such factors as his stage of artistic development, his psychological and socio-economic status, and his environment.

Few elements akin to the travesty are evident in the *Erzählungen*, formerly entitled *Moralische Erzählungen* (1752). Sentimental, perhaps rather than "moral" in nature, they neither idealize nor scorn virtue or antiquity. They are rather gently moralizing vignettes which are set in some exotic place, real or imaginary. Their kinship to the narratives woven into James Thomson's *The Seasons* (1726-1730) is manifested in spirit, setting, and meter, rather than by similarities of plot elements. As the English work which had inspired Wieland, they uniformly lack dimension and color, wit and humor, qualities which characterize Wieland's later work. Gruber reminds us that the rhymed *Erzählungen* were composed before Wieland had become acquainted with the *Contes* by La Fontaine, the frivolous *Schäfererzählungen* by Rost, or even Marmontel's *Contes moraux* to which the *Erzählungen*, at least on the surface, seem to bear some resemblance. Choice of motifs, as well as the qualities of lightness, rusticity, demure mischief, and occasional tearfulness are reminiscent of their precursors. The poet was aware of the weaknesses and immaturity of his early opus. By invoking the Horatian *beatus ille* motif Wieland's introduction set the tone indicative of his poetic nostalgia for an "ideal" past which may well refer to the vitality and purity of antiquity, rather than of his own life. The chronology of his works convinces the reader that this mood—a vestige of his heritage and earlier education—did not prevail.

Balsora, the first tale of the *Erzählungen*, is based on a prose account in Addison's *The Spectator*. Only a few of Wieland's departures from his model have relevance to this study. For example, he presented the insensitive, authoritarian father as a tyrannical, cruel caliph. In contrast with the English source, he showed little concern for material matters. The erotic element, however, is emphasized as the driving power in the plot development. Still, the tone is devoid of wit and sarcasm, and the spirit of *Empfindsamkeit* dominates. In an early manifestation of *Diesseitsfreudigkeit*, Wieland was determined to see a pair of separated lovers happily united in this life, rather than in the hereafter, as the source rationalizes. Unlike the original pair's rigidly controlled monastic existence, Wieland's lovers never even entertain the thought of celibacy, in spite of their despair. His gentle disposition rejected rigidity, especially that of ascetic monasticism (*cf. Sixt und Clärchen*, and *Die Wasserkufe*). He chose to counteract the bitterness of disappointment with magic which enlivens the sober prose of the original and, by method of simulated death, allows the heroes to be spared for a joyful life together. Wieland facilitated their nocturnal escape from the pompous palace where they lay in state by providing an apathetically superstitious environment—perhaps his most direct thrust.

Another more prominent narrative within this cycle, *Zemin und Gulindy*, shows affinity to Milton's *Paradise Lost*, Canto IV. The account involves the maturation process and eventual alliance of the two princely characters, under the guidance of a special mentor: Firnaz, a bucolic genius with a hand in fate, is a kindly attendant spirit to young nobles, a zealous champion of *Tugend*, and perhaps a forerunner to Oberon who, however, is the product of a more mature artistic mind. Wieland's blank verse in iambic pentameters portrays Gulindy's emotional experiences which accompany her physical development, her erotically colored speculations and introspections. Gulindy's first perceiving her mirror image in the water is modeled after the passage in Milton in which Eve sees her reflection. Milton's Eve, the "mother of human Race," reservedly relates the incident, while Gulindy actively experiences it in self-conversation, a device calculated to involve the reader. Wieland is less edifying than his venerated model. He devoted considerably more space to Gulindy's personal sentiments which he saturated with sentimental oxymora. Gulindy—a more human Eve—is well aware of her charms. Her rhetorical question, "Allein für wen sind alle diese Reitze?" (II, 92) suggests flirtatious qualities compared with the lines of Milton's Eve who concedes, "How beauty is excell'd by manly grace / And wisdom, which alone is truly fair" on being led to her "other half."[1]

Beyond these scant, juvenile manifestations of a rare poetic gift to be refined in future works, the *Erzählungen* represent a compromise between an as yet vague personal inclination and the taste of a revered standard—Bodmer.

Even a polemic product of this stage in Wieland's development, his *Ankündigung einer Dunciade für die Deutschen* (1755), reflects its measure of *Empfindsamkeit*. As self-appointed spokesman for the Swiss, Wieland intended an indictment—à la Pope's *Dunciad* against Gottsched and his followers, the inflated literary dunces. The *Ankündigung...* had been prompted by the anonymous *Die ganze Aesthetik in einer Nußschale, oder Neologisches Wörterbuch* (1754) by Freiherr von Schönaich, of the Gottsched persuasion. At this point, Wieland had not yet attained the subtlety which marked and tempered his expression in later works. While the occasion afforded a superb opportunity for satire, we find instead a factual, pugnacious accusation with merely a sporadic sampling of irony.

By 1758 much of Wieland's sentimentality had given way to

increased psychological insight and the factor essential to the travesty—irony. His intimate friendship with the socially adroit Zimmermann, the ultimate estrangement from Bodmer, attempts at dramatic production, and especially the reading of Helvetius, Swift, Lucianus Samosatensis, and Ariosto, contributed to the process of molding the ardent spiritualist into a skeptical cosmopolite. The poet's newly widened horizon, a legacy of the remainder of his Swiss epoch, predisposed him favorably for his rôle in Biberach.

Count Stadion's illustrous court at Warthausen offered Wieland a welcome escape from the futility of his administrative post in Biberach. The liberal, enlightened spirit which pervaded the Warthausen circle sustained him through animating intellectual and social diversions during the professional and personal adversities of his tenure in his native town. Thanks to her husband's influence at the Warthausen court, Sophie La Roche remained Wieland's trusted intermediary. It follows that the taste and demands of so prominent a patron as Count Stadion would superimpose themselves on the receptive protegé and recent "convert." While the poet's surrender to Stadion's ideals was not so unconditional as it had been to those of Bodmer, there is evidence of his indulging the count's fancy with morsels of a decidedly naturalistic character. The period of exposure at Warthausen and his sensitive awareness of Stadion's preference for erotically colored subject matter in literature and in the arts was of inestimable consequence to Wieland's development as a writer of travesties.

Under the influence of the prevailing spirit—a degree coarser than the French Rococo—his hitherto underdeveloped or perhaps suppressed penchant came to the fore. To be sure, the commissioned nature of the literary products, the recency, indeed, the relative precipitance of Wieland's social "assimilation," and his own artistic immaturity, among other factors, stigmatized his work of this stage (*cf.* Sengle, pp. 172-173). Undeniably, this segment of the poet's production is marked by a predominance of sensuous motifs which occasionally border on the risqué. Basic to them all are the playful frivolity and the pastoral guise of themes borrowed from antiquity, as the titles and names suggest. The characteristic superficiality—a noted trademark of the fashionable *rien*—stemmed in part from his ambition to emulate the French *legereté*. His adaptations of this time impart the poet's striving for this ingredient fairly rare in German literature; yet, they also reflect his lack of adequate perspective in successfully relating the factors essential to a work of consequence. Curiously, at the same time this incongruous quality nurtured the evolution of the genre with which this study is concerned. The demand for light and witty literature in the mundane, anti-Platonic vein, tersely narrated, and preferably culminating in a clever *pointe*, naturally fostered the travesty. Wieland was glad to oblige—in German—in itself a feat rare to Count Stadion whose ear up to that time had been atuned mainly to French euphony. "...[*Aurora*]... hat sogar meinen alten ehrwürdigen Protektor, den Grafen von Stadion, von seinem wohl hergebrachten Vorurtheile wider die deutsche Poesie bekehrt; er wunderte sich gar zu sehr, daß man das alles in deutscher Sprache sagen könne..." (*cf.* letter to Geßner, dated October 8, 1764. *DB*, I, 22-23).

Beyond the literary contribution, Wieland's social rôle in the intimate circle of Warthausen fulfilled another mutually beneficial function: the refreshing mingling of the commoner-humanist's philosophy with that of the court, in spite of the inevitable distance and the incidence of differences. Peripheral as the products of this period may be considered in Wieland's work as a whole, they deserve credit for his pioneering spirit in a growing effort to bring superior quality to the German poetic expression even in lesser genres. Ironically, his oft censured, unduly reactionary leaning behooved his progress as a master craftsman in the genre of the travesty.

The *Komische Erzählungen* (published in 1765) which began to originate in 1762 under the aura of Warthausen bear a stamp of frivolous insignificance. In most of his adaptations of this period, the erotic element plays a dominant part. *Diana und Endymion* (1762), inspired by Lucian, irreverently treats the love adventure of a lascivious goddess. In *Das Urtheil des Paris* (1762) Wieland not only echoed but amplified the ironical tone of his antique model, Lucianus Samosatensis, by leading his disrespectful provocations to the point of *piquanteries*. His travesty calls in question the unimpeachable majesty of the ancient goddesses, the virtue of impartiality in judging a contest, and the honesty in awarding the prize to the winner. Furthermore, he disputed the purity of love which, in this apparently rigged, divine beauty contest functions as a "bargaining" agent. The presence of some archaisms in isolated instances (*e.g.* "beut") may indicate an effort on Wieland's part to approximate the atmosphere of his model. On the other hand, the uncommon, colorful exclamation in direct discourse ("'Beym Styx...'") which occurs repeatedly throughout the *Komische Erzählungen* constitutes a humorous paradox: while implying a definite "regional," traditionally gloomy frame of reference, the mood of the passage is hardly stygian in character.

The lack of pathos in treating a subject involving deity, and the undue familiarity with which the poet and his mortal hero deal with goddesses are, of course, a trademark of the travesty. Wieland's propensity for diminution clearly extended not only to volume but also to the appraisal of the stature of the exalted—be it immortal or mortal, tangible or intangible. Traditionally awe-inspiring personages, institutions, and values—perhaps disproportionately revered—were taken down a notch or so by Wieland. Compelled by his widening horizon, his growing cosmopolitanism and resulting increased *Menschenkenntnis*, he felt inspired, if not equal, to the challenge.

These poetic overtures to a genre in which he excelled eventually are of considerable significance to German literature in spite of their shortcomings: the depersonalized, carefully devised mutation of popular, adaptable motifs was an aesthetic adventure hitherto rarely or inadequately undertaken. Results of previous attempts at scornful adaptations reflect too heavy a hand and perhaps too sharp a tongue in their zeal to reveal the obvious intention (*cf.* Chapter II). Other adaptations of exalted themes were more or less consistent in according the subject matter the customary heroic treatment (*cf.* Georg Rudolf Weckherlin's version of the divine competition). Even though Wieland's goddesses probably served as an allegory for influential noblewomen, he did well to steer clear of personal satire. An exception to this practice may be seen in *Juno und Ganymed*, a work containing some profane allusions to exalted womanhood, and one which Wieland ultimately rejected (*cf.* Sengle, p. 174).

Aurora und Cefalus is based on Ovid's *Metamorphoses*, VII, entitled *The Story of Cephalus and Procris*.[2] This source was a favorite mythological subject for pastoral Rococo and Classicism. Wieland undoubtedly appreciated Ovid's tearful *Rahmenerzählung*. Common to both narratives are Cefalus' love for his wife Procris, Aurora's interest in Cefalus, and her intrigue to alienate the couple's affections. The motif of the test is employed once more. The goddess's successful efforts of bending Cefalus' ear lead to the hero's gnawing doubts about Procris' absolute steadfastness in the face of temptation. Wieland introduces a bit of magic to his travesty: a ring which has the power to grant favors is instrumental in changing Cefalus' identity in the scheme of weakening Procris. Wieland again departs from Ovid who brings about the couple's reconciliation. When at the critical moment Cefalus reveals his true identity to Procris, she leaves in a fit of resentment, and the hero, afflicted with misgivings, tries to follow and find her. Irony plays a substantial part in Wieland's ancient model as well as his own rendering of the account. Ovid castigates suspicion, inquisitiveness, and precipitance, and lets the hero live and suffer. His Procris, reconciled, presents her husband with a dart which, ironically, becomes the weapon of her ultimate murder by her mate. During a hunt he hears a rustle in a bush from where Procris, made suspicious by a misleading rumor, had tried to spy on Cefalus; he throws his dart, fatally wounding his beloved wife, and himself becomes a victim of grief and remorse.

Gruber calls attention to various versions of this narrative, and mentions the influence of Ariosto and La Fontaine on Wieland's resolution of the plot.[3] By reversing the jealousy theme he finds room for additional frivolity. In his search of Procris, Cefalus locates her in the intimate company of

Seladon whose identity Cefalus had recently borrowed. Downcast at her infidelity, Cefalus resolves to drown himself in the lake where Aurora happens to be bathing at the time; she saves him by kissing him back to life. The tone which prevails in Wieland's version deliberately fails to convince the reader of Cefalus' genuine state of dejection. When his weak constitution and hurt pride drive him to contemplate suicide, Wieland refuses to let him extricate himself so easily. Besides, the previous occurrence of the fantastic element and the superficiality of the hero's convictions cause the reader to anticipate a resolution other than tragic. Not only is Cefalus "condemned" to live, but he is resurrected by the scheming personification of Eros. Ovid's account of the involuntary manslaughter and its haunting consequences to the unfortunate survivor elicits compassion at the end. Wieland's treatment, on the other hand, ignores the presence of profound sentiment in any of the persons involved, which provides the farcical character that is typical of many of his earlier works in this genre. His humorously reproachful reference to La Fontaine regards the corruptibility of "virtue":

> Hans La Fontain, nun sagt mir noch einmal,
> Der Kassenschlüssel sey der Schlüssel zu den
> Herzen!
>
> (VII, 94)

Throughout the cycle of the *Komische Erzählungen* the poet seems to be making a sport of his travesty. In *Aurora und Cefalus*, adjudged superior to the other accounts, there is evidence of growing refinement. Count Stadion's approval not only sanctioned the method but also the quality of his "court poet's" workmanship. With the advent of these products Wieland in effect emancipated the German parodistic literary tradition from its heavy didacticism (*e.g.*, Dedekind's *Grobianus*), while guarding against cynical immoderations (*e.g.*, Nicolai's *Die Freuden des jungen Werthers*). He, indeed, set the tone for the social acceptance of certain "improprieties" on the condition that they were "decently" presented. The novelty of his literary "deportment" roused indignation among many of his fellow *literati* and critics who objected to his accomplishments as offensive excursions into obscenity (*cf*. Sengle, p. 176). Not until decades later have literary history and criticism vindicated Wieland, yet, without ever fully crediting him for his unique contribution. The poet's own commentary concerning his achievements in this genre is scant. As a result of the generally unfavorable critique of the *Komische Erzählungen*, however, he attempted to pass them off as essentially moralistic products, that is, as satirical portrayals of the social mores prevailing in the *beau monde*. From the tone of his correspondence on this matter with Salomon Geßner and subsequent concessions one may conclude that Wieland himself was not thoroughly convinced of the moralistic message of the *Komische Erzählungen* (*cf*. letter to Geßner, dated January 5, 1767, *DB*, I, 52 f). Later, on the occasion of a new edition of the *Komische Erzählungen*, Wieland called Friedrich Just Riedel's attention to some modifications in the text—apparently a compromise which the poet regretfully regarded as a concession: "Sie sehen, wie viel ich dem Geschmack und der *honnetété publique* darin aufgeopfert habe" (letter, dated June 2, 1768, *DB*, I, 189).

Wieland's further evolution as a poet, especially with regard to his development in the parodistic vein, is colored by incisive personal experiences which profoundly affected his philosophy and expedited the maturation process: The ill-starred love for the socially unequal Christine Hagel, his Shakespeare translation (1762-1766), his conventional marriage to Anna Dorothea von Hillenbrand (1765), and finally, the controversy with Count Stadion, which was reconciled only shortly before the count's death (1768). Wieland's growing stature as a translator and an author of renown (*Die Abenteuer des Don Sylvio von Rosalva*, 1764; *Die Geschichte des Agathon*, 1766/67) accelerated his desire for personal and creative independence. The differences with La Roche, and Wieland's spitefully patriotic attitude in an administrative feud over the relocation of a mill according to Stadion's wishes were nominal causes of the break with Warthausen; the real reason was Wieland's increasing awareness of the painful inequality between the members of the serene court and the commoner civil servant — no matter how prominent. His subsequent, slighting treatment of ruling figures derived its roots—in part—from this episode, and was later compounded by the influence of the Weimar period. Conversely, the poetic shaping of his *humanitas* gained immeasurably from the impact of the discord.

In a letter, dated August 29, 1764, Wieland informed his editor Geßner of the nature and model of his *Musarion*, a verse narrative which was in preparation at that time but which was not published until 1768 (*AB*, II, 251). He announced a humorously didactic poem according to the manner of Matthew Prior's *Alma, or the Progress of the Mind* (1718). This rhymed dialogue in three cantos, an elaboration on existing speculations concerning the soul—its abode and its fate after death—aimed at reducing the "authoritative" claims to infallibility made by respective, contradictory interpretations. Even though the rationalistic concept of his model was not acceptable to Wieland at this stage, he welcomed its emotional quality and its quest for balance over extremes. He spoke benevolently of the spirit prevailing in his source while castigating some of the more radical, contemporary moralists: "...davon bin ich sehr überzeugt, daß die Priors und Hamiltons des vergangenen Jahrhunderts liebenswürdigere Leute waren, als die feyerlichen stoischen moralischen Sauertöpfe unserer Zeit," he said in a letter of July 10, 1766 to Zimmermann (*AB*, II, 266).

Wieland conceived of his own poem as "...ein ziemlich systematisches Gemisch von Philosophie, Moral und Satyre..." (*cf.* letter to Geßner, dated July 21, 1766, *DB*, I, 33). Indeed, Wieland's satire invades the sphere of philosophy as he proceeds to expose two extremists whose human weaknesses had been mantled by the aura of their mere membership in their respective school of philosophy—further proof that Wieland was not wont to accord his characters the immunities traditionally pertaining to representatives of revered institutions, purely on grounds of their station or professed conviction. The protagonist himself is saved from extremism through the delightful and useful, thoroughly human teachings of the charming Musarion. Her own philosophy is less than lofty, her method of instruction may not be orthodox, but it succeeds in imparting the ideal of amiable balance. In a letter, dated Warthausen, March 15, 1769, Wieland assured his friend Weisse that Musarion's spirit is really an articulation of his personal philosophy, as he put it, "ich bemühete mich, Musarion zu einem so vollkommenen Ausdruck... [meines Geistes] zu machen, als es neben meinen übrigen Absichten nur immer möglich war. Ihre Philosophie ist diejenige, nach welcher ich lebe; ihre Denkart, ihre Grundsätze, ihr Geschmack, ihre Laune sind die meinigen. Das milde Licht, worin sie die menschlichen Dinge ansieht; dieses Gleichgewicht zwischen Enthusiasmus und Kaltsinnigkeit, worein sie ihr Gemüt gesetzt zu haben scheint; dieser leichte Scherz, wodurch sie das Überspannte, Unschickliche, Schimärische... auf eine so sanfte Art... vom Wahren abzuscheiden weiß; diese sokratische Ironie... diese Nachsicht gegen die Unvollkommenheiten der menschlichen Natur—welche... mit allen ihren Mängeln doch immer das liebenswürdigste Ding ist, das wir kennen" (this letter was intended as an introduction to a new edition of *Musarion*, as the poet informed Riedel on January 19, 1769. Cf. *DB*, I, 247). The fact that Wieland chose not to alter the form of the verse narrative of his model, technically excludes *Musarion* from consideration under my delimitation. Yet, the spirit reflected in the above letter seems to illustrate his attitude concerning matters exalted and the ideal of balance— circumstances which seem to justify the reference.

In 1771 Wieland undertook to rework the old Syrian tale *Kombabus* which the sophist-satirist Lucian had incorporated into his treatises on the Syrian goddess, adapted from the Greek by Wieland under the title *Von der syrischen Göttin*.[4] In his *Vorbericht* to *Kombabus*, Wieland's editor J. G. Gruber invites the reading public to compare the original (in Wieland's translation) with his new version. It is amusing to perceive Gruber's attempts at advertising Wieland's latest opus, so to speak, and at the same time his endeavors to glorify the poet's efforts in lending dignity to this fairly risqué motif of antiquity. Gruber maintains that few of the world's tales combine all ingredients essential to a fascinating poetic narrative more successfully than this old Syrian tale, and he praises Wieland's sense of propriety and tact in handling this motif. In the editor's appraisal, the poet succeeded in his delicate treatment by providing the hero's unusual deed with a nobler motive than did Lucian (VII, 149-150). Wieland's tendency to ennoble a deed by giving it the aura of a sacrifice which necessarily requires a high degree of self-denial is later observable, for example, in his *Oberon*. Sengle submits that *Kombabus* was published in 1770, and he points out the relationship among this work, *Aspasia* (1773), and the *Komische Erzählungen;* this relationship, he maintains, consists in the frivolity of the plot elements. Indeed, in his selected edition of 1784 Wieland had incorporated *Aspasia*, and *Kombabus* "mit den drei salonfähigsten komischen Erzählungen unter dem Titel 'Griechische Erzählungen'" (Sengle, p. 176). Sengle takes exception to Gruber's views: "Gruber... rückt den 'Kombabus' weit vom französischen Rokoko ab. Dennoch will mir scheinen, daß die 'Zucht und Delikatesse' der Behandlung, ihre Ironie, die philosophische Einleitung, die Einfügung eines edlen Beweggrundes für die Tat, die gepflegte Sprache und was man sonst noch rühmen könnte, den ursprünglichen naturalistischen Charakter des Stoffs und seine Widerlichkeit nicht aufzuheben vermag! Hier gelangte Wielands Formkunst an eine Grenze, welche für die Ästhetik nicht uninteressant ist, insofern im 'Kombabus' die Bagetellisierung des Stofflichen... besonders anschaulich ad absurdum geführt wird" (Sengle, pp. 176-178).

Here, too, Wieland's concern with virtue, and mild-mannered didacticism are constituent elements in his travesty. The poet himself labeled *Kombabus* an *Erzählung*, and attached to its title a subheading in the form of a rhetorical question, *Was ist Tugend?* The philosophical introduction to the rhymed iambic work abounds in references to Greek history and mythology, and in allegory. The opening lines assimilate the stock phrase of the French Rococo, *je ne sais quoi*, with a sarcastic reflection on the nature of virtue:

> Die Tugend ist, wenn wir die alten Weisen
> fragen,
> Ich weiß nicht was—Laßt's euch von ihnen
> selber sagen!
> Dem einen Kunst, dem andern Wissenschaft,
> Dem ein Naturgeschenk, dem eine Wunderkraft;
> Der Weg zu Gott, nach Zoroasters Lehren;
> Der Weg ins Nichts, nach Xekia's Schimären.
> Sie ist, spricht Pyrrho, was ihr wollt;
> Und mir, schwört Seneka, noch theurer—als
> mein Gold;
> Sie ist der wahre Stein der Weisen,
> . . . .
> Doch wohl im Traume nur, ruft Spötter Lucian
> (VII, 151-152).

Wieland's poetic version differs from the prose original in a number of ways. The latter is an *Ich-Erzählung* by a "native Assyrian," partially an eyewitness account, partially a renarration of a tale told by the priests. From a complex background involving the famous temple of Hierapolis, the Syrian "Holy City," its founders, deities, and diverse theories of origin, eventually evolves the actual Kombabus plot. Wieland's version, on the other hand, starts *in medias res*. Lucian's queen Stratonika is charged by Hera in a dream with the responsibility of erecting the Hierapolis temple in her honor. As a punishment for ignoring the goddess's request, the queen is taken seriously ill; only then she imparts her negligence to the king who makes immediate preparations for her journey to Hierapolis. Here it is clearly the king's initiative that precipitates action, not the queen's persistent nagging, as is the case in Wieland's account. In the latter, a king whose name ends in "-us" is blessed with a beautiful, young, resourceful wife, Astarte. Wieland expounds the prominent theme of impiety and expiation while slighting the patron goddess of matrimony in a disparaging parenthetical expression: Queen Astarte had vowed to appease the goddess by personally undertaking a journey to a distant country, "Der Schützerin (doch nicht dem Muster) guter Frauen / Den schönsten Tempel aufzubauen" (VII, 154).

When the aging king politely suggests the possibility of delegating the execution of the terms of her promise, Astarte cleverly refutes his rationalizations, and finally resorts to acute illness. Here Wieland observed an opportunity to inject his lines with witty fatalism and *Menschenkenntnis:*

> Ein weiser Mann von sechzig zweifelt immer,
> Traut wenig eurer Weisheit zu,
> Und eurer Tugend nichts
> (VII, 156).

The unfortunate Kombabus, the king's confidant and favorite, is asked to escort the queen on her unusual pilgrimage, command troops, and supervise the building project. He begs to be spared the superhuman responsibility in view of the constant exposure to the presence of the queen and resulting inevitable problems. Overruled by the king's insistence, Kombabus requests seven days in which to settle his affairs. "Unselige Reise, deren Ausgang ich nur zu gut voraussehe! Ich bin selbst noch jung und werde einer schönen jungen Frau zum Begleiter gegeben. Unfehlbar wird mir das größte Unglück daraus erwachsen, wenn ich nicht sogar die Möglichkeit des Übels, das hier zu besorgen ist, aus dem Wege räume. Ich muß mich zu einem großen Opfer entschließen, wenn ich aller Furcht entbunden sein will. Dieser Entschließung zufolge verstümmelt er sich selbst..." (Lukian, 355). In his rhymed verse travesty Wieland dramatized Lucian's factual report. The king entrusts the queen to Kombabus' care for two years, and promises him half his crown upon faithful execution of his mission. This exaggerated reward in itself underscores the element of distortion. Having learned that the sexagenarian holds little stock in virtue and is, furthermore, opposed to his consort's uncommon pledge requiring a lengthy separation, the reader is invited to question the validity of the promised, oversized compensation. The attitude of the hero, too, differs from that of his ancient model. Wieland's Kombabus does not dare voice his reservations, let alone protest: He is the faithful reincarnation of the courtier who knows better than to disappoint his illustrious patron, and to invite the latter's wrath along with his own doom. The poet goes on to illustrate his appraisal of favoritism practiced at courts in his own time:

> Nun sagt, was konnt' er thun—als was er
> schweigend that?
> Sich tief bis auf den Boden bücken,
> . . . .
> Mit Worten sattsam auszudrücken,
> Versprechen, schwören,—kurz, was jeder Günstling
> muß,
> Mit Lächeln heuchlerisch des Herzens Kummer schminken,
> . . . .
> Kombab entfernet sich
> (VII, 157-158).

Wieland paralleled his model in his hero's dilemma and solution through sacrifice. He also retained the further plot development: the emasculated hero deposits a small sealed treasure chest containing the ultimate proof of his innocence with the king for safekeeping, and departs with the queen and her retinue. Soon, the queen falls in love with her retainer. In spite of her frustrations Wieland's Queen Astarte is subtly played down in comparison with her model, Stratonika, whose passion drives her to intoxicate herself in order to facilitate her confession to Kombabus, and to dramatize her demands by suicide threats. In either case, the object of the queen's attention finally confesses the cause of his apparent aloofness, and in both versions the rumor of the "illicit relationship" reaches the distant king's ear. Wieland, however, retarded the action by extending the royal separation for another year. This seemingly insignificant modulation of the time element serves to reduce the rashness and with it, the violence, of the passions while directing the emphasis on the tribute to the goddess. Lucian's hero is recalled at once, and views his return with confidence, "...weil er seine Apologie zu Hause gelassen hatte" (Lukian, 358); Wieland's counterpart is even more at ease:

>...Der Bau ist nun vollendet,
>. . . . .
>Und, weil man nichts was sich gebührt
>Vergessen will, das dritte Jahr geendet.
>Der König, dem ich weiß nicht was oft schwer
>Ums Herze macht, betreibt den Rückzug sehr.
>Nicht daß er sich die Zeit indessen nicht vertrieben!
>   (VII, 175).

Upon their return to the royal court the "culprits" face a veritable inquisition. Here Wieland is obviously relishing the courtly intrigue:

>Merkur mit Flügeln an den Sohlen
>Vermöchte nicht den Höfling einzuhohlen;
>So groß ist die Begier, aus pflichtgemäßer Treu
>Dem alten König zu berichten,
>Wie nah' Kombab mit ihm verschwägert sey.
>Wißt ihr wie Höflinge in solchen Fällen mahlen?
>Die Farben werden nicht dabei
>Gespart, das glaubet mir!...
>...Ein Kerker schließt, so bald sie angekommen,
>Astarten und den Günstling ein
>   (VII, 176-177).

While Lucian's king factually accuses Kombabus of the threefold crime of adultery, contempt, and sacrilege, Wieland again with succinct pointedness takes to task the hypocrisy of the collective, narrow-minded *Tugendbolde*:

>"Welch Aergerniß!—So kann der Schein
>Der Tugend uns belügen!"—schrein
>Aus Einem Ton die Spröden und die Frommen.
>. . . . .
>Indessen fährt der König fort

> Die Schaar der Zeugen zu verhören,
> Und hundert Augenzeugen schwören,
> Man sah sie tausendmal allein, wenn Zeit und Ort
> Die Sache sehr verdächtig machten:
> . . . .
> Was sie gethan, ist—was man schließen mag!
> Denn freilich konnte man so nah hinzu nicht gehen
> Um alles auf ein Haar zu sehen
> (VII, 177-178).

Once again, the amelioration of the conclusion in Wieland's version constitutes the essence of his travesty. When the ancient Kombabos [sic] is sentenced to die he finally breaks his silence with the overt assumption that he is being put to death not because of his suspected grievous offense but because of the king's greed for the treasure in his safekeeping. The tension is resolved when both the content of the chest and Kombabos' shortcoming are revealed, much to the horror of the king. From this discovery on, Kombabos stands once more in the highest royal grace. He returns to complete the unfinished temple construction, and has many followers. When on learning of his unfortunate condition, a passionate beauty actually commits suicide, Kombabos resolves to avoid further heartbreak by wearing female attire henceforth. This ends the original Kombabos episode *per se*, though not the treatise on the Syrian goddess. Wieland's Kombabus ignores any side issues or extraneous deliberations. His only concern is to prove the queen's and his innocence by producing the evidence; he, too, is reinstated into the king's graces. The narrative ends with a devastating thrust at Kombabus' fellow courtiers who are eager to emulate the favorite by following his example:

> Die Wuth sich zu kombabisiren
> Ergriff sie insgesammt. In kurzer Zeit bestand
> Der ganze Hof aus einer Art von Thieren,
> Die durch die Stümm'lung just das einzige verlieren,
> Um dessentwillen man sie noch erträglich fand
> (VII, 182).

The humorous coinage of an original euphemism (the reflexive verb *sich kombabisiren*) tends to temper the naturalistic impact and the echoes of bitterness in this passage—a compact reference to the political and social impotence of contemporary courts, and a drastically sarcastic derision of courtly mores, rivalry, and vogue, no matter in what respect.

Lucian's work is already pervaded with irony, which appealed to Wieland, and he enlarged upon it liberally. Most of the changes which he undertook occur in psychologically "strategic" moments. He deliberately expanded certain ideas in order to underscore the satirical element, and with it his social critique and implied didactic message. In spite of the numerous objections to its risqué nature, Wieland's *Kombabus* is an excellent example of the poet's ability to travesty by lending the elegance of his language even to compositions involving themes of questionable taste.

Wieland's preoccupation with the past, as illustrated, was not confined to antiquity. Chivalric themes, specifically motifs reminiscent of the Arthurian cycle, have engaged his interest and become nuclei for some of his most colorful adaptations. *Das Sommermährchen* (1777) is a verse narrative in the setting of the chivalrous world. Gruber cites a "fabliau" by Chrétien de Troyes as Wieland's source. An adaptation entitled *La Mule sans Frein* appears in the February 1777 volume of the *Bibliothèque Universelle des Romans*, and in Pierre Jean Baptiste Legrand d'Aussy's *Fabliaux ou Contes du douzième et du treizième Siècle*, I (1779) based on a collection of 1756. In this tale Wieland exhibits a pleasure which he derived from the naive (Sengle, p. 353). In that spirit, and in recognizing the incredibly limited and totally inadequate stock of existing children's literature, Wieland had entertained the idea of entitling his tale *Kindermährchen*. The thought that out of one hundred readers eighty might have their feelings hurt discouraged him, however. Indeed, while many fantastic elements might justify its classification as a children's tale, its fine irony and rare artistry of versification defy such an apparent limitation, but not its designation as a travesty.

The perilous disenchantment of a fairy castle as a test of

chivalrous love and courage is the main theme of this tale. Again, Wieland followed the plot outlines of his model. A pretty lady whom Wieland calls Genevra arrives at King Artus' court on muleback. The court is assembled at Carduel for the feast of Pentecost according to the original. Wieland initially makes the point that it is spring, and he uses the season, not the feast, as the source of joy. He idealizes the quality of humility at courts of old while lamenting the blasé attitude of the more decadent, hypersophisticated, contemporary courts:

>Als einst zur Morgenstunde
>Fürst Artus lobesam
>an seiner Tafelrunde
>sein Frühstück nahm:
>da stand mit ihren Frauen
>die Königin
>im Erker, auszuschauen
>ins Grüne hin,
>und sich zu freuen
>des holden Maien.
>. . . . .
>Da war noch gute Zeit, ihr lieben Leute,
>da man bei Hofe sich an so was freute!
>   (XXI, 217-218).

The lady in distress is bemoaning the theft of her mule's magic bridle. She enlists the aid of the Round Table in the search for the missing, treasured item. Wieland modified the solemnity of her promised reward—her lifelong devotion—by introducing a humorous variant:

>. . . . .
>gelob' ich feierlich,
>wie's ihm beliebt,
>entweder—abzutreten
>das Maul,...[having magic attributes]
>...oder—ich

> will all mein Lebelang allein
> zum Dank sein treues Liebchen seyn
> (XXI, 221).

Herr Gries, Wieland's counterpart to the ludicrous messire Queux, is a braggart, harum-scarum, and a coward to whom the idea of personal gain appeals more than that of a noble deed.

In both versions, the respective author attests to the magic attributes of the mule, but Wieland's wording attains farcical character in this passage:

> Sein Thier, ein Eselein
> von Feenart,
> bracht' ihn in Ja und Nein
> an einen Wald
> (XXI, 227).

His perplexing adventures with a thousand lions, a dragon, and an all too narrow bridge—the third obstacle to the enchanted castle where the bridle is to be found—easily persuade Gries to give up. While the French Queux hides in embarassment on his return, his German counterpart boasts of the dangers he successfully withstood—a living travesty of the ideal of a noble knight.

The second part has the parallel adventure of Gawin for its subject. The young noble has returned, and has eagerly offered the distressed lady his services. Wieland's language reflects the magic of the atmosphere, while the tone becomes increasingly parodistic:

> Der Mond schien hell
> zu seiner Reise;
> sein Maul, nach Feenweise,
> lief vogelschnell.
> . . . .
> und wie der erste Morgenstrahl
> die Welt illuminirt,

> entdeckt das Schloß sich seinem Blicke,
> . . . .
> Herr Gawin war dem Zaudern gram.
> Er denkt: "Wer sich den Teufel zu verschlucken
> entschlossen hat, muß ihn nicht lang' begucken..."
> (XXI, 238-239).

After innumerable combats—true to form—Gawin is escorted to the fairy, a sister of the unfortunate maid, who reigns over the palace and guards the bridle. The latter is invested with the power of bestowing eternal youth, beauty, and charm. Gawin realizes that these attributes would mean more to the palace fairy than her wealth and power which she tyrannically exercises over the subjects in her domain. Having only his mission and honor in mind he valiantly withstands her pleas, even as she resorts to bribery, and succeeds in obtaining the bridle. In contrast to the French source wich hails Gauvain [sic] as a redeemer, Wieland chose to complicate the plot by playing on the fairy's psyche: as she watches Gawin depart with the magic instrument of her youthful loveliness, she is unable to bear the grief—a mixture of wrath and sorrow and an excellent device for enhancing the comic touch—and she commits suicide. The model *fabliau* concludes with the return of the bridle to the maiden, her verbal show of profound gratitude to the knight, and her solo departure on muleback. The subtle didactic message in Wieland's version involves the issue of the kept promise on the part of both parties concerned—the claimed reward on fulfillment of a condition. As the deliberately exaggerated, purely external effect of the magic bridle becomes visible, Wieland enlivens the assembled, perplexed court by endowing its members with some genuine properties of human nature on the occasion:

> Sie war vorher schon hübsch zu nennen,
> doch itzt vor lauter Schönheit kaum
> noch zu erkennen.
> Die Damen und die Ritter sahn

> Sie neidisch—Ihn mit Mißgunst an.
> Allein Herr Gawin lacht,
> Komm, Liebchen, spricht er, laß uns wandern!
> nimmt flugs mit einer Hand den Zaum,
> das Mädchen mit der andern,
> und gute Nacht!
> (XXI, 264)

The brisk exit, and the striking psychological and stylistic finesse render *Das Sommermährchen* a first-rate travesty sure to appeal primarily to a sophisticated audience.

After a considerable interval Wieland composed his last verse narrative, *Die Wasserkufe* (1795). In a letter, dated January 9, 1795 to Herder, the poet himself referred to his fleeting poetic "Renaissance" as an "etwas eilfertige[s] Kindlein meines grauen Alters" (*AB*, IV, 36). As in the earlier *Komische Erzählungen* he had parodied classical mythology, he now extends his banter to the Christian world (*cf. Sixt und Clärchen*, 1775, and *Klelia und Sinibald*, 1783).

Wieland's model was the prose account *Du Prévot d'Aquilée* in Legrand's *Contes Dévots pour servir de Suite aux Fabliaux et Contes du treizième Siècle*, according to Gruber. While the plot parallels the original fairly closely, Wieland's spirit is less than *dévot*. He seems to relish rendering the clumsy recluse's unrehearsed experience with "temptation" in the person of the senechal's wife. Indeed, the poet subtitled the narrative *Der Einsiedler und die Seneschallin von Aquilegia*, partially following the original. The brief introduction contains a gently moralizing appeal to all solid "pillars" of society:

> "Wer fest auf seinen Füßen steht,
> Der sehe zu, daß er nicht falle!"
> Die Warnung, lieben Brüder, geht
> Euch an und mich, und, ohne Ausnahm', alle...
> (XXII, 263).

The narrator of the *Ich-Erzählung*, maintains "audience contact," so to speak, by frequently addressing himself to the readers through apologetic, acquiescing, or explanatory phrases. His relationship to the recluse is a direct, personal one: Bruder Lutz's character and predicament are grasped and credibly portrayed with psychological insight. Wieland's idiom achieves a satisfying balance between a measure of *Volkstümlichkeit* and pointed ironical critique. As the unnamed hermit of the source, Lutz in his isolation has lost contact with the secular world, and arrived at the dangerous belief that few men on earth equal him in merits. While the original recluse asks God to reassure him in a revelation, Wieland's hero in all his *Treuherzigkeit* is less humble, although the poet is quick to blame Lutz's meager diet for the *Eigendünkel* so unbecoming his station. Not by request, but as a stern warning, he experiences a vision advising him of a meritorious example of true virtue in the person of a man dedicated to the highest ideals and serving God in his own way. The presumptuous hermit sets out to encounter the man who rivals him in virtue, and to find an opportunity of testing his own. He receives from the departing provost a symbolic ring recommending him to the wife and house of the provost in the latter's place, with all privileges. Lutz soon learns of the literal meaning and inclusive nature of these privileges, and eventually of the intended moral. Wieland's humor immeasurably adds to the image of the overly zealous hermit who naively associates luxury with lust, and, suddenly exposed to the worldly splendor of the provost's household and consort, seriously doubts that such can be the abode of virtue: "... 'In diesem Hause / Lebt alles ja in Saus und Brause!...'" (XXII, 268). The hermit compounds his *hybris* by questioning the purpose of his mortifications in contrast with the plush convenience of pleasing God with superior results. Wieland articulates Lutz's private thoughts in direct discourse with God, as does his model; however, he does not miss a stab at the church hierarchy:

> Von Gold und Silber, Elfenbein
> Und Marmor schimmern alle Wände;
> Das Hausgeräth glänzt wie polirter Stein;

> Für einen Erzbischof wär' hier nichts zu gemein,
> Auch nimmt der Diener Zahl kein Ende
> (XXII, 269).

During his brief sojourn the hermit learns that it takes indeed more stamina to remain "pure" in the face of temptation. He hears that his beautiful hostess and her husband are bound by a voluntary vow made in a moment of supreme peril, to total abstinence for seven years. The guest, as part of his trial, is exposed to many aspects of temptation, beginning with culinary stimuli. Reluctantly he resists in order not to be shamed by his hostess. He is less successful in restraining the passion which the lady's close proximity arouses in him when, according to the privileges granted through the ring, he finds himself reclining next to her. Wieland capitalizes on the issue of temptation, a form of a test and a frequently employed theme in his work. The very title of the tale refers to the basin into which the attractive *Seneschallin* dunks him repeatedly whenever immodest desires come upon him. The basin was built by the provost for his own use and identical purpose for the duration of the vow.

Wieland renders to the reader an articulate account of Lutz's struggle with his passion, his conscience, and his hostess who maintains perfect control of the situation. The poet, however, ignored the original hermit's sanctimonious claim that he permitted such involvement merely to test the powers of the ring. Wieland's preoccupation with erotic motifs has tenaciously continued to occupy a sizeable portion of his repertory, in spite of his many vacillations, his increasing maturity and resignation. In incredibly rich variations, the erotic element keeps reappearing—ever dominant, colorfully costumed, but not indecent, compelling but not importunate, and a superb instrument of the travesty. The impertinence of the design and the intended lesson notwithstanding, Lutz's trepidation is understandable, as well as comically pitiable. His relative frankness occasioned by lack of polish and exposure to the ways of the world redeems his figure. Wieland's hermit draws chuckles, but he is not a laughing stock, and much less a caricature. The literal cold baths which he receives on top of the figurative ones—the lady's reprimands—humble him, and send him, considerably meeker, back to his modest abode. The conclusion metaphorically illustrates the deflation of a nature-oriented hermit:

> [Lutz]...kriecht in seinen Pilgerrock,
> . . . .
> Und wandert nun, viel weniger gebläht
> Als da er kam, mit manchem Wurm in seiner Seele
> Und manchem Pfahl im Fleisch, nach seiner Bärenhöhle
> (XXII, 296).

His penitence seems to rest in the subdued withdrawal from the sphere of further temptation, unlike the ardent *confietor* of his model who mortifies himself so as to merit a place in paradise. No serious thought of atonement enters his implied *mea culpa*, let alone any concern with his fate in the hereafter. His temporal experience extends to the matter of retribution—and he has, after all, suffered for his presumptuousness. Wieland completes his travesty by letting the chastened rustic off without spiritual castigation.

It appears that the somewhat naturalistic, often coarsely comical world of the *fabliau* held considerable attraction for Wieland in various stages of his literary career. His travesties which are based on these products of a past tradition reflect refined wit and psychological finesse along with plot adaptations of universal appeal.

2

THE FAIRY TALE

An overwhelming portion of Wieland's travesties involves the fairy tale as a model. Almost throughout his literary career an affinity to the fantastic element is peculiar to

Wieland; it is likely to pervade his narratives in verse and prose, and to engage his thought in theoretical treatises. In fact, I have demonstrated repeatedly how he used fantastic guise to considerable advantage in his travesties as a mitigating agent.

In spite of his exposure to the *Sturm und Drang* and his resulting attempts at *Volkstümlichkeit,* Wieland could not even remotely be associated with the folk tales such as those transmitted by the oral tradition and ultimately collected and edited by the Brothers Grimm. A characteristically pre-Romantic, rational atmosphere prevails in the *Volksmärchen der Deutschen* by Johann Karl August Musäus (1782-1786), a friend and contemporary of Wieland. The older, enormous French collection, *Le Cabinet des Fées* (1785-1789) is similarly imbued. This quality was undoubtedly conditioned by the time, as Schneider reminds us: "Unter dem bestimmenden Einfluß des Zeitgeistes steht vor allem Wielands Märchendichtung. Sein Märchen liegt weit ab vom romantischen, das ...sich in Waldeinsamkeit verliert oder in das geheimnisvolle Walten dämonischer Mächte. Sein Märchen taugt aber auch nicht für den Volksmund und nicht für die Kinderstube" (Schneider, *Barock-Klassizismus*, p. 250).

It was the refined fairy tale of the *Feen-* or *Zaubermärchen* variety which intrigued Wieland. Strangely, the font of German tales held little appeal for him. Instead, he turned to themes from the more cultivated world of antiquity, of French, and Italian fairy literature, of exotic Oriental tales, especially of the *Arabian Nights*, chiefly in the French translation by Antoine Galland (1781-1785).

By virtue of his artistic adaptations of numerous fairy tales Wieland scored a double triumph: while excelling as a leading exponent of the travesty he became a prominent pioneer in the area of the *Kunstmärchen* at the same time. To Wieland the fairy tale as a genre radiated fascination. If the *Aufklärung* in its obsession with the principle of verisimilitude and its timidity toward the marvelous had little use for the inexplicable, fantastic realm, the Rococo spirit delighted in polished products involving such "frivolities." As a champion of the fairy tale, Wieland attested to the impact and circulation of narrators of the fantastic genre: "Unter allen Schriftstellern hat der Fabeln- und Märchendichter den weitesten Kreis. Alle Alter, Geschlechter und Stände, junge und alte, hohe und niedrige, gelehrte und ungelehrte, beschäftigte und müssige Personen versammeln sich um den Erzähler wunderbarer Begebenheiten und hören mit Vergnügen, was sie unglaublich finden..." (Wieland, XXX, 5). He further submitted that wit, esprit, and even philosophy of an esoteric nature can be successfully harmonized with the fairy tale, which was destined to become a unique medium for the expression of his *humanitas*.

The "Rococo" fairy tale was by no means the sole monopoly of a youthful consumership. The attractive illusion of the tale was called upon to elicit the imagination and to provide vicarious —not rarely frivolous—experience for educated persons of good taste. Most of Wieland's products in this genre have little to offer to the immature. His emphasis on the erotic, the frequently complex plot elements, and the elegant language replete with colorful rhetorical devices, indeed, the very tone itself endear him chiefly to a sophisticated audience. Although he did not reject the plain tone of the more primitive children's and folk tales, it had no place in his work even though there is evidence of occasional attempts at popular expression. The poet recorded his concern for the niveau of the fairy tale as a literary genre. He expressed regret at the unduly large number of artistically inadequate products and poor imitations of certain weak originals which should not be a part of a reputable collection of fairy tales. Such products, he felt, "...müssen Werke des Geschmackes sein, oder sie sind nichts. Ammenmärchen, im Ammenton erzählt, mögen sich durch mündliche Ueberlieferung fortpflanzen, aber gedruckt müssen sie nicht werden" (Wieland, XXX, 9). Aesthetic considerations of this nature seem to point to Wieland's critical appraisal of the quality of the products of others, as well as his own artistic adaptations.

In his previously cited essay *Über den Hang der Menschen an Magie und Geistererscheinungen zu glauben* (*cf.* Chapter II),

Wieland justified the realm of the fantastic as the most fecund source of a poet's products and interests. He pleaded the case of phantoms, genii, goblins, water sprites, in short, of all fantastic supernatural beings, friendly or detrimental, for he knew that these spirits and their disputed existence will continue to occupy a considerable corner in literature and in the hearts of most men.

> Selbst der aufgeklärtere Theil der Menschen—Personen, die es auf keine Weise von sich gesagt wissen möchten, daß sie Gespenster, Gespenstererscheinungen, und was in dieses Fach gehört, im Ernste zu glauben fähig wären—unterhalten sich doch gern mit Gesprächen oder Lektüren dieser Art.
> ...Eine Tradizion, die so alt als das Menschengeschlecht, oder doch gewiß um viele Jahrhunderte älter als die Filosofie ist, hat eine Art von allgemeinem Glauben und Einstimmigkeit aller Völker über diese Dinge hervorgebracht. Von Kindheit wird unsre Einbildungskraft mit Bildern, Mährchen, und angeblichen Geschichten angefüllt, welche sich auf diesen Glauben gründen und ihre ansteckende Kraft an uns beweisen, zu einer Zeit, da wir uns noch keines Betruges versehen, und die Vernunft uns noch mit keinen Waffen gegen unsre eigne und fremde Leichtgläubigkeit ausgerüstet hat (XXXII, 125-126).

The essay mirrors Wieland's dichotomy. While affirming man's craving for the sublime and the marvelous, an esoteric awareness of a mysterious obscurity ("heiliges Dunkel") which not every one is privileged to penetrate (XXXII, 128), the poet appealed to reason as a check and balance. In the fairy tale particularly, Wieland revealed the extent to which he was capable of harmonizing apparently contradictory streams of thought, as well as the degree of independence which truly creative minds always assert. As cognizant as he was tolerant of human weakness and the sensations and inclinations which form a substantial part of our bliss, he invited men to beware of perilous deceptions. Man's penchant for the supernatural, his belief in "invisible bears," as he called it, and his desire to know more than he can and, indeed, is supposed to, Wieland called man's "schwache Seite." He cautioned his readers to be on guard against any dangerous deceit by appealing to reason and experience.

In another essay, *Über die vorgebliche Abnahme des menschlichen Geschlechts* (1777), Wieland contended that each civilization in the earlier stages of its evolution has passed through a fabulous and heroic age of demigods, giants, and heroes, from which poets later have drawn a wealth of material. To this heroic age Wieland attributed a potency, physical and moral wholesomeness, indeed, sensitivity, which he lamented to be lacking in his time: "...unsre alkoholisirte und so oft nur affektirte Empfindsamkeit, die wir voraus zu haben glauben, ist nur ein schwaches Surrogat für die lebendigen, starken, voll strömenden Gefühle der Natur" (XXXI, 226). In the same essay Wieland advocated poetic expression which reflects "...Natur, Einfalt und Wahrheit über Künstelei, Flitterstaat und Schminke...," but he rejected "...Ungeschliffenheit und...Cynismus..." which he resented as typical of the "Modeton" of his time (XXXI, 247).

Except for the two accounts in the *Dschinnistan* collection (1786-1789), for which Wieland claimed originality, his fairy tales were adapted from more or less prominent sources.

In 1772 Wieland called on the sumptuous world of the *Arabian Nights* to incorporate certain elements in his political novel *Der goldne Spiegel oder die Könige von Scheschian*. The irony in his tone demonstrates his genuine attitude toward the perpetuation of the fairy tale and the absolute monarchy —in an exotic frame. "Alle Welt kennt den berühmten Sultan von Indien Schach-Riar, der,...alle Nächte eine Gemahlin nahm, und alle Morgen eine erdrosseln ließ, und der so gern Mährchen erzählen hörte, daß er sich in tausend und einer Nacht kein einziges Mahl einfallen ließ, die unerschöpfliche Scheherezade durch irgend eine Ausrufung, Frage oder Liebkosung zu unterbrechen,..." (XVI, 19). In the introduction he satirizes generations of ruling monarchs as personifications of intellectual inadequacy. His portrayal of the court philosopher, Danischmend, bears autobiographical traits, for Wieland himself was a kind of court philosopher whose flights of fantasy were often censured by the Duchess Anna Amalia and her court.

In the *Geschichte des weisen Danischmend und der drei Kalender* (1775) Wieland continued to glorify the figure of Danischmend as an unpolitical philosopher-idealist, exiled from the glittering world of the court to which his services have become useless. He has fallen from grace with the ruling monarch for trying his patience, and for failing to reconcile his own philosophy with that of the ruler. The incident is reminiscent of Wieland's retirement as the tutor to Karl August from the court of the principalities of Weimar and Eisenach. The increasing alienation between the poet and the Duchess Anna Amalia lead to his eventual dismissal from this position. Into this prose work Wieland incorporated his version of an episode beginning with Night XXVIII of the *Arabian Nights*, entitled *The Story of the Three Calendars, Sons of Kings; and of the Five Ladies of Bagdad*, in the French translation of Galland. As in previously cited examples, Wieland's portrayal of the three calendars—members of a sect of wandering mendicant dervishes—ignored their physical peculiarities, and centered instead on their mental and moral makeup. Unlike the royal, uniformly one-eyed calendars of the source, Wieland's counterparts have the tinge of socially and morally deficient specimen: parasites, idlers, and swindlers. In Chapter 6 he first introduces one of the calendars who serves more or less as Danischmend's partner in a conversation concerning domestic tranquility. Chapter 8 of the novel is entitled "Geschichte der drei Kalender" (XVIII, 42 ff). Here Wieland concentrates his biting critique of the trio's objectionable activities, as well as the mental and cultural shortcomings of those whom the calendars are out to victimize, the dense populace of Lahore. In this episode Wieland again seized the opportunity to disparage the worthless members of even a semireligious order that would condone their fraudulent "missionaries" in their illicit pursuit of revenue which handsomely defrays their own expenses. By demonstrating their questionable methods Wieland voiced indignation at the calendars' craftiness in the art of preying upon the gullible plebeians. The eldest, most experienced of the three indeed enjoyed ill-gotten prosperity as he elaborates: "Was für ein Geheimniß besitzt ihr, diese tauben Ottern von Lahor zu beschwören, daß sie euch mit dem Mark ihres Landes mästen?—Geduld, sagt' ich: du sollst es sehen. Es ist die leichteste Sache von der Welt, die Mildherzigkeit dieses Volkes zu besteuern. Der ungeschickteste Strohkopf hat dazu Geschicklichkeit genug..." (XVIII, 46-47). In Chapter 12 and in successive chapters, the contemptible character of the first calendar, Alhafi, is further revealed. He entered the order because he had no talent or ambition for anything else; his opinion of humanity is distorted because for thirty years he has been a mere spectator (94). The wise Danischmend is clearly the antidote to the negative, insensitive calendar. In due time the worst of Alhafi's characters comes to the surface: he intrigues against Danischmend, and all three calendars, reunited, seek to ruin the philosopher, bringing about his exile, war, devastation, and their own total debauchery, until the tide turns, and Danischmend is happily reinstated. Compared with his source, the three key figures undergo pejoration in Wieland's version: their birth, their traits and experiences are debased, so as to depict a detrimental element of society within the framework of his political novel. The insertion of a fairy tale into such a prose work of major stature may be attributed to the immense popularity of fairy tales at the time, as well as to the fictitious, exotic setting of the scene. The somewhat static tone observable in Galland's translation in this tale and others is enlivened by Wieland's colorful invectives and metaphors, as I have shown.

The verse narrative *Das Wintermährchen* (1776) is based on two well-known tales from the *Arabian Nights*. Wieland's original title combines two parts, "Der Fischer und der Geist," and "Der König der schwarzen Inseln" under one heading. The charmingly sarcastic, rhymed prologue lends a frame to the narration. It exposes at once the narrator's, Scheherezade's, rare story telling talent which has successfully staved off her doom. At the same time it anticipates another complacent sultan, a superb character distortion which bears Wieland's trademark and is reaching almost prototype proportions in this work.

> Mein Schwesterchen, sprach Dinarzade,
> Wenn ihr nicht schlaft, (denn um den Schlaf wär's
> Schade!)
> Erzählt uns doch, weil's noch so dunkel ist,
> Der schönen Mährchen eins, die ihr...
> ...so lebhaft zu erzählen
> Und sonderlich so gut zu dehnen wißt.
> Des Sultans Hoheit hat die Gnade
> Und hört euch, zwischen Schlaf und Wachen,
> gerne zu:
> Denn was sein Herz dabei empfindt
> Wird seine Seelenruh
> Nicht unterbrechen.
> Schach Riar gähnt: Das will ich euch versprechen!
> Und seine junge Frau beginnt
> (XXI, 163-164).

Indeed, the almost invariably negative treatment of the Oriental potentate constitutes a major factor of Wieland's travesty in contrast with his source. On the one hand, Galland, whose sovereign was the absolute monarch Louis XIV, seemed to retain the same awesome respect for divine authority as his Islamic original; therefore, the figures of the sultans are treated in a tone becoming their prestige or at least in a neutral manner. Wieland, on the other hand, appeared to delight in allotting more lines to the potentates and their ways, so as to allow himself to indulge in sharp criticism of irresponsible rulers. In the following passage Wieland's sultan echoes the *carpe diem* attitude of the original prose, only much more eloquently, as the monarch departs on a secret fact finding mission to satisfy his curiosity:

> Den Leuten, die etwa nach mir fragen,
> Ist leicht was scheinbars vorzusagen;
> Bald hab' er Halsweh, bald Kolik,

> Bald Podagra, bald Krampf im Magen.
> Regiert im übrigen mit Glück!
> Verschiebt so viel ihr könnt auf morgen;
> Sorgt immer für den Augenblick,
> Und Gott laßt für die Zukunft sorgen
>   (XXI, 185).

Another striking deviation from the source is Wieland's modification of the character of the genie, and that of the fisherman. Sengle notes a marked rise in the "gefühlsmäßige Element" (Sengle, p. 347). He senses in the doggerel of this work the influence of the *Sturm und Drang*, and an attempt on Wieland's part at simplifying his style; it demonstrates, says Sengle, "die Absicht des Dichters, deutscher und herzlicher zu dichten, ... Im Vergleich mit ihrer Quelle fehlt der Wielandschen Erzählung alles Raffinierte und Komplizierte....die Erzählung ist schlichter und knapper geworden; auch die Sätze sind einfacher und kürzer....[Es] wird hier das biedere Reimpaar des Knittelverses angestrebt" (Sengle, pp. 346-347).

The despair of Wieland's poor fisherman is convincing through the primitive terms of his ejaculatory prayer. In his dealings with the genie, he has no occasion to resort to trickery. As a balancing agent we perceive a measure of skepticism in the humble fisherman startled by the supernatural phenomena:

> Wie geht dieß zu? Gott steh' mir bei!
> Es ist doch wohl nicht Zauberei?
>   (XXI, 170).

Wieland's genie whom the fisherman liberates from the vessel is a straightforward, reasoning—but not coldly calculating—"human" being. Having remained true to his convictions, and wronged by intrigues, he shows no vengeful appetite upon his deliverance, but merely gratitude and compassion with the fisherman. His motives, manner, and diction make him far more congenial than his original counterpart. Contextual changes are slight.

In the second part of the narrative Wieland suspended the initial gravity of the situation by injecting wit and punning into the king's affliction. As a result of a curse pronounced by his wicked consort the unfortunate, young king of the Black Isles is petrified from the waist down, and doomed to this pitiful existence amid seemingly lifeless splendor of his enchanted palace and environment. He shares his lament with the visiting sultan:

>   "
>   . . . .
>   Geholfen kann mir nimmer werden!
>   Mein Elend ist so wunderlich,
>   . . . .
>   Unglücklich durch alles, was ich fühle,
>   Unglücklicher noch durch das, was ich
>   Nicht fühle!"
>   Der Sultan denkt bei sich:
>   Dem müssen wahrlich die Wörterspiele
>   Geläufig seyn, der übel sich fühlt
>   Und noch mit Gegensätzen spielt!
>   (XXI, 192).

Compared with Wieland's colorful, lively metaphors, Galland's French prose reflects the sobriety of a public ledger: "...elle prononça des paroles que je n'entendis point, et puis elle ajouta: 'Par la vertu de mes enchantemens, je te commande de devenir tout à l'heure moitié marbre et moitié homme.' Aussitôt, seigneur, je devins tel que vous me voyez, déjà mort parmi les vivans, et vivant parmi les morts...."[1] The sultan who resolves to free the unfortunate noble is, to be sure, an eager avenger, but he operates without thinking. His impetuous pursuit of the evil, adulterous queen culminates in the apprehension and instant execution of her and her black lover. Absurdly, the queen was the only one who could have revoked the curse.

At this point Wieland departed from the source plot in order to intensify his travesty. While in the original fairy tale the queen's death means automatically the king's deliverance and happiness ever after, Wieland introduced a *deus ex machina* in the shape of the jackass's head which is said to possess magic powers, and at the same time lends itself as an instrument of ridicule as the standard of the royal house. Wieland's sarcasm goes so far as to elevate the ludicrous bogey to a symbol of redemption by means of such predicates as *groß, edel*, and even *heilig*.

> Weil nun an diesem besagten Schädel
> (Wie eine alte Sage ging)
> Das Schicksal unsers Hauses hing:
> So könnt ihr denken, wie groß und edel,
> Ja heilig, darf ich wohl sagen, gar
> Der Eselskopf dem Volke war.
> . . . .
> Er hatte die große Eigenschaft,
> Durch seine bloße Gegenwart
> Alle Bezauberung aller Art
> Mit allem Geister- und Feen-Wesen
> Auf einmal gänzlich aufzulösen.
>   (XXI, 210-211).

Cognizant of its miraculous powers, the late queen had had it sunk into the sea so as to make the enchantment complete. In order to effect the king's recovery, the sultan proclaims a reward for the priceless, lost skull. Popular reaction varies from public indifference to cautious skepticism among the enlightened few:

> Die Leute schütteln mächtig die Ohren:
> "Was geht der Eselskopf uns an?"
> Ich sorge, denkt mancher weise Mann,
> Der Sultan hat den seinen verloren
>   (XXI, 213).

The poor fisherman rejoices, for he had raised the seemingly worthless item from the sea. Contrasted with the happy end of the original tale, Wieland deglamorized the conclusion of his version. There is no evidence that any of the parties involved lives happily ever after. With the deliverance of the king everything around him returns to realistic normalcy once more, and there is not much fascination to the routine of everyday life:

> Die Fische werden zu Bürgern wieder,
> Wimmeln die Straßen auf und nieder
> Bei Sonnen- und bei Mondes-Licht,
> Des alten Schlenders unvergessen;
> Haben viel Müh und karg zu essen,
> Bau'n Tag und Nacht viel Böhmische Schlösser
> Ins Blaue hinein, hätten's gern besser,
> Und rathen immer und treffen's nicht:
> Kurz, alles ist wieder in seiner Pflicht
> (XXI, 214).

In Wieland's adaptations of the fairy tales there seems to be as little preoccupation with the "ever after" as there is with the hereafter elsewhere in his work. Plausible, if disenchanting resolutions which—unlike those of the original fairy tales—reestablish the *status quo*, no matter how bleak, are rather the rule in Wieland's fairy tale modulations.

The source for his verse narrative *Hann und Gulpenheh oder zu viel gesagt ist nichts gesagt* (1778) provides a plot of sensational impact with a sobering *pointe*. Wieland's adaptation of the Turkish *Forty Viziers* contained in the *Bibliothèque Universelle des Romans*, II (Paris, October, 1777) closely parallels his model. His subtitle, *Eine morgenländische Erzählung*, somewhat deemphasizes the eccentricity of its unique plot elements. Wieland's *Groteskkunst* here rests in the skillful intensification of the characters' deliberately exaggerated emotions. His verse heightens the effect of the doting young couple's manifestations of mutual affection. The poet chuckles at their intense rapture, their disproportionately earnest reaffirmations that one could not go on living without the other—should they be parted by death. Wieland made a special point of the wife's unsolicited effusive vows that she would gladly be buried alive with her husband in order to escape the fate of living without him, a fate worse than death. The device anticipates the *méchante* Gulpenheh's depravity. Soon her untimely demise occasions Hann to live up to his promise as he loudly laments his loss at her grave. Moved by the unfortunate widower's grief the prophet Aïssa brings about Gulpenheh's resurrection from the dead and the couple's boundless felicity. Hann insists on fetching her clothes in order to return her home appropriately attired. No sooner has he left, the son of the king passes by the cemetery where the inadequately garbed Gulpenheh is to await her husband's return. The prince is overwhelmed by what he sees, and Wieland capitalizes on the situation:

> Der Königssohn macht Halt,
> Und nähert sich allein der reizenden Gestalt,
> Die, um zum wenigsten den Busen zu verzäunen,
> Genöthigt ist den Alabasterglanz
> Von zwei untadeligen Beinen
> Der Lüsternheit der Männeraugen ganz,
> Wiewohl erröthend, Preis zu geben.
> Der Königssohn...
> Verschlingt das schöne Weib mit seinen Blicken schier
> (XXII, 255).

He wraps her in his own coat, and after duly inquiring as to her marital status, proposes to make her grace his harem. The tailor's wife recognizes His Highness and the inestimable value of such an association. Without hesitation she disowns her lawful husband, and is eager to become the prince's "obedient slave." On his return Hann has occasion to lament the second loss of his beloved wife. After months of useless search he learns by coincidence of his wife's whereabouts, and charges to the palace, demanding her return. The prince insists that he was unaware of the existence of a lawful husband. Wieland, it seems, cannot tolerate a purely noble, innocent monarch, and imparts to the reader the idea that the tailor's arrival is not unwelcome to the prince who has already tired of Gulpenheh's charms. In a confrontation of the spouses, Gulpenheh commits the incomparable effrontery of identifying the tailor as a criminal who robbed and left her stripped at the cemetery. Upon such devastating testimony the tailor is sentenced to hang. It is the appearance of the venerable prophet Aïssa whose true account of the story saves the tailor from ruin.

In the tone of the conclusion Wieland differs from his source which renders an unemotional report. He achieves dramatic effect by cleverly exposing providential power and resulting instant reward and punishment. His emphasis is on verbs into which he manages to pack the full force of his irony, hinting at the appraisal of Gulpenheh's moral values without the benefit of descriptive adjectives:

>...Aïssa hoch geehret
>...spricht mit Profetenmacht;
>Herbei wird Gulpenheh gebracht;
>...Von ihrer Schuld gedrückt
>Hebt sie die Augen auf, erblickt
>Den Wundermann, und sinkt entseelt zu seinen Füßen.
>   Hann wird mit Gold und Ehren überhäuft,
>Frau Gulpenheh ins Grab zurück geschleift;
>Dort mag sie bis zum jüngsten Tage rasten!
>Ihr lieber Mann fühlt keinen Drang
>Im Herzen mehr, nur neun Sekunden lang
>Auf ihrer Gruft zu weinen und zu fasten
>   (XXII, 260).

Here Wieland acknowledged poetically the unwholesome presence of such universal characteristics as amorous folly, zealous status covetousness, and the resulting evils of sudden, undue social rise. In spite of some of the crass plot elements, his version, in Sengle's words "wird... dem Bereich zynischer Satire entrückt und zum Beweis eines Weltbildes, das darum humoristisch ist, weil es um die Unzulänglichkeit des Menschen ...weiß. Wieland malt die heiklen Situationen der Geschichte nicht lüstern und boshaft aus, ...aber er macht auch nicht den kompromißlerischen Versuch, dem derben Stoff eine idealistische Seite abzugewinnen. Er begnügt sich ...mit einer kongenialen Wiedergabe der tollen Novelle, denn eben dadurch, daß ihre Komik so massiv, so übertrieben ist, wirkt sie nicht peinlich" (Sengle, p. 356).

Another aggressive satire of an Oriental monarch—and for that matter any autocratic, demented ruler—is *Schach Lolo, oder das göttliche Recht der Gewalthaber* (1778). The source is *The Story of the Grecian King and the Physician Douban*, which is inserted as one of the genius's narrations in the *Story of the Fisherman, Arabian Nights*.

The original story begins at once after a matter-of-fact introductory statement concerning the Grecian origin of the king's subjects: "Il y avait au pays de Zouman, dans la Perse, un roi dont les sujets étaient grecs originairement."[2] Wieland, on the other hand, indulges in a politico-philosophic chat in iambic meter, evidently to justify the subtitle:

> Regiert—darin stimmt alles überein—
> Regiert muß einmal nun die liebe Menschheit seyn,
> Das ist gewiß! Allein—
> Quo Jure? und von wem?...
> Gewöhnlich fing man damit an,
> . . . .
> "Sich vörderst in Besitz zu setzen."
> Das Recht schleppt dann, so gut es kann,
> Sich hinter drein...
> . . . .
> Das Jus Divinum, liebe Herrn,
> Steht also, wie ihr seht, so feste
> Und fester als der Kaukasus:
> "Befiehlt wer kann, gehorcht wer muß;"
> . . . .
> So wird die Welt regiert, und eine ganze Fuhre
> Von Syllogismen macht's nicht mehr noch minder wahr
> (XXI, 315-316).

The sarcastic tone of the subtitle certainly finds an echo in the above elaboration. Having set the stage, Wieland proceeds to illustrate the dissolute character and life of the sultan, an irresponsible sovereign who left the business of government mostly to the gods and fairies, that is to say, to chance. A ludicrous routine of lavish waste and utter ostentation characterizes his Epicurean "Quasi-Leben." Wieland suggestively cites the opulent way of life as the cause for the sultan's consuming affliction with leprosy. At last the fabled physician Douban comes to his aid and succeeds in curing him within seven days. Mindful of his promise, the sultan upon recovery makes Douban his favorite, until the evil, prejudiced grand vizier influences the monarch against the new favorite. The wicked design assumes dangerous dimensions, and the sultan, having eventually yielded to the convincing propaganda, decrees that Douban must die. Wieland had found a rather labile, easily influenced character in his model. He continued, however, to weaken him further by underscoring not only major but also minor foibles which, ironically, turn out to be fatal. The sultan's curiosity is centered on one of Douban's books containing vital questions to be answered by his head upon decapitation. The execution and instructions are carried out, and the king eagerly turns the pages to satisfy his hunger for the sensation to come. Wieland makes the point that Lolo, among his other shortcomings, cannot turn a page without moistening his finger. This relatively insignificant fault proves to be his ruin, for the pages were saturated with poison. Grotesquely, Douban walks away with his head but not without directing a few parting words at the dying sultan. While the physician's preachment is of a moralizing nature it does not echo the vicious vengeance of the wronged in a final triumph over the wrongdoer who is reduced to a wretched state. Again, Wieland's conciliatory spirit prevails.

One of the most artistic products in the category of fairy tale adaptations—Goethe's favorite—is *Pervonte oder die Wünsche* (1779). This charming poetic miniature reaffirms Wieland's assertion concerning the negligible artistic value of printing "...Ammenmährchen, im Ammenton erzählt...." The old Neapolitan nursery tale, an extract of which appeared in the *Bibliothèque Universelle des Romans* (June and September

1777), challenged the poet's imagination. Its naive tone, but apparently also its promising intricacies invited "refashioning." The travesty lies mainly in the elevation to carefully wrought lyrics of a comical, primitive prose tale, and in the humanization of its characters.

Again, the distortion remains limited to mental and moral attributes. Wieland's Pervonte, the hooligan son of a poor widow, is a redheaded "Kauz" with a rich variety of "Kruditäten," who does not share all the absurd asymmetry of his model's features. A "Flegel,...fein warm und dicht in— Dummheit eingehüllt..." (XXII, 8), he nevertheless incurs the gratitude of three fairies whom he had protected from sunburn by fashioning a shelter, presumably for his own amusement while loafing in the woods. As a reward the fairies invest him with the power of having his every wish granted, and vanish. By means of this popular fairy tale theme Wieland seized the opportunity of exposing human folly, and censuring the deplorable lack of conservation, humility, and common sense, especially at court. The constant abuse of a fantastic privilege —the instant gratification of every wish, no matter how nonsensical or even villainous, is richly illustrated. With refreshing humor Wieland candidly unfolds some fairly brazen situations not commonly found in genuine fairy tales, for example, Pervonte's bizarre, mischievous wishing the haughty Princess Vastola pregnant by him in retaliation for having publicly ridiculed him. When the unsuspecting princess gives birth to twin daughters, Wieland welcomes the chance of unleashing his biting sarcasm against the bourgeois hypocrisy of his and any society on such occasions:

> Der inhaltsschwere Blick, das Zischen hinter Fächern,
> Das Aergerniß der tugend- ehr- und zucht-
> Begabten Raths- und Bürgersweiber:
> Der Jungfern Angst vor gleicher Wassersucht;
> . . . .
> Dieß alles, und was jedermann
> Bei einem solchen Fall moralisiren kann...
>   (XXII, 14-15).

The monarch being taken to task is Vastola's father, the scandalized king of Salerno. Determined to learn the intricacies surrounding the disgraceful incident, he is willing to try the "psychological" approach after seven years of fruitless queries: the twins are spontaneously to identify their father from respective crowds of nobles and commoners invited for the purpose. When the children fly into Pervonte's arms the paternity case is closed and the infamous family tossed out to sea in a keg by the outraged king. Noble Vastola is characterized as an extravagant, superficial, and scheming shrew who uses her husband's extraordinary gift to her own advantage. She is aware of his limited reasoning powers, and sees the need of cleverly formulating his wishes. Physical and material comforts are the prime consideration; first, their lot in exile is improved by exchanging the keg for a magnificent palace as a residence. With material worries out of the way, Vastola now wants Pervonte to become physically attractive. At this point, Vastola's model feels compelled to set matters straight by insisting on a legitimate marriage. A chaplain is summoned to bless the matrimony. Wieland's princess, on the other hand, has no misgivings: to her the union is a purely erotic experience. Only when the novelty wears off she makes renewed demands. This time, she has him wish for intellect, ironically disregarding the possibility that, once so endowed, he would reason independently and assert his will against hers. Pervonte, as does his model, actually becomes enlightened. His first act in the new state of mind is to urge contentedness. The laudable exercise of his newfound faculties to a positive end, his moral awareness, and especially the quality of humility constitute the lesson in the original fairy tale. In keeping with the tradition of the genre, the hero is richly rewarded. A life of tranquility, and reconciliation with the king who, overjoyed by providential vindication of Vastola's innocence, installs the family to succeed him, guarantee a happy "ever after."

Wieland departed from his source chiefly through a twist of Vastola's character, a device which retards and mutes the happy ending. His princess becomes bored amidst the convenience of wishing more conveniences. She relieves the monotony of their *Schäferleben* through parties, new lovers, and satisfies her urge to tease her father by dropping in and disappearing from his court at festival time. Pervonte now represents reason and a block to her whims, yet a necessary instrument. The fairies are being plagued ceaselessly. So as to allow her to continue her stylish travels without Pervonte she demands one final wish as a parting present: a perpetually full purse. Pervonte is in agreement; he himself begs the fairies to grant his last wish: to return everything to the status quo. Here Wieland illustrates the triumph of humility and the punishment of greed, since this final wish extends also to Vastola—but not at pain of preachment. Wieland is neither a pure moralizer nor inclined to make a serious case of his *Feerei*, as I have shown. His concept of the issues in his version is reflected in the resolution—which in itself qualifies as a travesty. He lets the wonderful world burst like a soap bubble, "Und—die Komödie ist aus" (XXII, 63). As Pervonte is returned to his original state the iambic meter confines itself more regularly to a simple doggerel. He voluntarily resumes his humble existence with but one gift—his functioning, able mind—remaining to him as a permanent, serviceable vestige. The modulation involving the power of reasoning was due to the influence of Herder and probably a regrettable echo of the *Aufklärung* (*cf.* Sengle, p. 358). While Pervonte has profited by the fantastic experience, Vastola—once more her father's darling daughter—is plagued with just enough memory of the fabulous episode to cause her discomfort. This is an incongruously magnanimous penalty imposed on a character so harshly castigated. The poet's tone lends *haut goût* to the *Volkstümlichkeit* which he found in his source; Wieland's humor, Sengle maintains, "nimmt...dem Moralischen und Bürgerlichen des Themas alle Peinlichkeit und Kleinlichkeit" (Sengle, p. 358).

Wieland's *Dschinnistan oder auserlesene Feen- und Geistermärchen* (1786-1789), a collection of fairy tales selected mostly from the French *Cabinet des Fées* (1785-1789) and adapted for German readers, was intended to meet the enormous demand for literary products in the fantastic vein. Of the twelve narratives contained in the collection Wieland himself claimed originality for only two, *Der Stein der Weisen*, and *Die Salamandrin und die Bildsäule*, which he incorporated into his works. Both prose accounts lack the color of Wieland's earlier, imaginative style. His former luster makes way for empirical subjects and a prosaic tone devoid of the witty *piquanterie* of earlier years. The aging poet had apparently lost his touch not only for the fairy tale, but also for the travesty. In both narratives the plot is resolved by rational means. Neither Wieland nor any secondary literature names a source for *Der Stein der Weisen* (1786). Its setting is in the frame of reference of the Artus legend, and features an uncomplimentary facsimile of King Mark of Cornwall. In the negative portrayal of this royal ruler and his court lies probably the only parodistic element in this tale. A weak character with less than noble traits traditionally unbecoming royalty, but typical of Wieland's usually negative portrayals of royal rulers, he was "hoffärtig ohne Ehrgeiz, wollüstig ohne Geschmack, und geizig ohne ein guter Wirth zu seyn" (XXVII, 51). He was also moody, gullible, and obsessed with a predilection for the mysterious, much to the profit of an impressive staff of parasitic "Wundermänner" who managed to nurture the king's curiosity for the precious stone, while cheating him unmercifully. The legendary philosopher's stone engages the king's imagination to a degree which is detrimental to his welfare: the sorcerer whose services he had greedily engaged to produce the substance of the precious stone vanishes, and His Majesty himself is turned into a jackass. His consort also fares badly: her lover, an unworthy knight, deprives her of her jewels, leaving her to be turned into a goat. In spite of some comical aspects Wieland's temperate prose fails to elicit even echoes of his past flippancy, and sounds magistral by comparison. The same shortcoming seems to be aimed at increasing the reader's awareness of the didactic message: a warning of the ill effects of overabundance, the heroes' eventual moral refinement, and their perception of a higher set of values, as well as their free choice to live by superior standards.

Die Salamandrin und die Bildsäule (1782) shows even less

parodistic intention. With the exception of a few features borrowed from the stock of Oriental fairy literature in French translation, Wieland claimed originality. Increasing sobriety had unfortunately replaced his aesthetic irony in this insipid product of an artistic crisis (Sengle, p. 406).

The volume of works discussed in my elaboration on Wieland's travesties of fairy tales reveals the extent to which he favored this inconspicuous genre as a source. While the current literary vogue undoubtedly influenced his choice, there is sufficient evidence in Wieland's own utterance, as well as in the assessment of scholars and critics that the poet was partial to the fairy tale. Its general character—the suspension of the laws of nature, its freedom from rigid adherence to established norms, its exotic flavor, and sometimes its plain naiveté—but especially the flexibility which it offers to the ironist, seems to have endeared it to Wieland. The extraordinary artistic niveau, chiefly the finesse of his verse travesties, is sustained testimonial to his successful preoccupation with his humbler models.

3

THE LEGEND

While Wieland was shown to have displayed notable affinity to themes from antiquity, to the Arthurian cycle, to French, to Oriental, and to other foreign sources which, by their nature might be considered "legendary," he seemed to be indifferent to the stock of German *Sagen*. The folk legend was not Wieland's métier. In view of his taste and his inclination for *Ausländerei*, it is amazing that he would make a naive German folk legend of the Eisenach area the object of one of his travesties.

In his *Der Mönch und die Nonne auf dem Mittelstein*[1] (1775), Wieland's *Einkleidungskunst* achieves a triumph through the artistic metamorphosis of a crude folk legend to a charming poem which seems to deride, as it were, the banality of its model.

In the prose preface to *Der Mönch und die Nonne auf dem Mittelstein. Ein Gedicht in drey Gesängen*, Wieland acquaints the reader with the legendary nature, the setting, and the source of the mutation which he had undertaken and which, in his opinion, needs no justification. The following comment refers the reader to the source of the plot itself:

> Neben der berühmten Wartburg stund vorzeiten auf einem hohen Berg eine Burg, die (nach einigen Chronicken) schon in der Mitte des fünften Jahrhunderts von einem von Frankenstein erbaut, 700 Jahre drauf von der Herzogin Sophia von Brabant während ihrer Händel mit dem Marggr. von Meissen, Heinrich dem Erlauchten, wieder aus den Ruinen gezogen worden, nun aber nur noch wenige Spuren ihres ehmaligen Daseyns aufzuweisen hat. Diese Burg hieß der Mittelstein, woraus der Nahme Mädelstein entstanden, den der Berg noch heutiges Tages in der Gegend führt. Auf diesem Mittelstein oder Mädelstein ragen zween ziemlich hohe Steine hervor, die von ferne, und in so fern die Einbildungskraft das Ihrige beyträgt, wie zwoo sich umarmende menschliche Figuren aussehen. Das gemeine Volk glaubte vorzeiten (und glaubt vielleicht noch) diese zween Steine seyen ein Mönch und eine Nonne gewesen, die aus wechselseitiger Liebe dem Kloster entsprungen und sich auf diesen Berg geflüchtet, daselbst aber zur Strafe ihres Verbrechens und andern ihres gleichen zum abscheulichen Exempel, in dem Augenblick, da sie sich umarmen und küssen wollen, in Stein verwandelt worden. Diese zu einer althergebrachten Sage gewordene Fabel konnte vielleicht zu nichts Bessern nutzen, als daß sie die Entstehung des gegenwärtigen Gedichtes veranlaßt hat. Aus einem solchen Mährchen kann ein Dichter machen was er will; er ist weder an Zeitrechnung, noch Costume gebunden; die damit vorgenommene [sic] Veränderungen bedürfen also keiner Rechtfertigung. Von der Fabel selbst aber kann, wer Lust hat, in Limperts lebenden und schwebenden Eisenach das Mehrere lesen (*T.M.*, III, 193-194).

In a brief, somewhat idealizing article, entitled "Wielands Gedicht 'Sixt und Klärchen,' sein ursprünglicher Plan und seine Quelle," Gotthold Klee theorizes that the legend which has since become perpetuated in the region of Eisenach was not popularly known at the time Wieland fashioned his verse narrative.[2] The poet, then, did not draw from "living tradition," Klee points out. Wieland's inaccurate bibliographical reference to the Limpert source, and a spelling or printing error in the alleged author's name—an error which persists through every existing edition—has long obscured the true identity of the work and its originator. The actual title of the source names Johann Limberg as collector and editor of *Das im Jahr 1708. lebende und schwebende Eisenach / Welches Anno 1709. zum Erstenmahl gedruckt und zusammen getragen worden von Johann Limberg / der Zeit Waisen-Inspector, Anitzo wieder übersehen und mit einem Curiosen Appendice vermehret. Gedruckt im Jahr 1712. Eisenach / verlegt und zu bekommen bey Daniel Christian Wilhelmi / Buchbinder*.[3] Klee further advises that according to A. Oesterheld, onetime Head Librarian of the Eisenach Library, the precursor to the Limberg source was *Das im Jahr 1708 lebende und schwebende Eisenach, zusammengetragen von Johann von Bergenelsen, einem Schwedischen* [von] *Geblüt. Gedruckt zu Stralsund, Anno 1709*, most of the copies of which were sent to Eisenach and made available there at Wilhelmi's bookbindery (Klee, 730).

Johannes Limberg (exact dates unknown), is reported to have led an adventurous existence as a student, soldier, teacher, and cleric. Among Limberg's more notable publications are his *Denkwürdige Reisebeschreibungen durch Deutschland, Italien, Spanien, Portugal, England, und Schweiz* (1690).[4] Formerly a Minorite Master of Novices, he converted to Protestantism in 1689—a circumstance which may account for his selection of the monastic topic and his slighting tone in the episode about to be examined.

Das im Jahr 1708. lebende und schwebende Eisenach... is an anthology of multifarious local color accounts rather than a systematic chronicle, incorporating descriptive as well as semistatistical prose concerning the city of Eisenach and its environment. Following an elaborate dedication to Wilhelm-Henrich, Hereditary Prince of Saxony, and Prince Carl August of Saxony, Limberg justifies his current opus through a reference to the learned English chancellor and historian, Verulamius, who in a treatise had encouraged the recording of noteworthy events not only at courts of nobles but also in less exalted strata. While Limberg's effort emulates the intention of his erudite example, his stylistic means are inadequate: the presentation suffers from limited vocabulary, faulty punctuation, indeed from lack of clarity or continuity. There is evidence of sententiousness, of objectionable taste—in short—crudity.

The account which served Wieland as a model is simply entitled *Der Mittelstein* (Limberg, pp. 273-278). Before relating the issue itself, the narrator provides a frame by means of an *Ich*-experience: while sight-seeing in the area, the castellan points out to him the Mittelstein, so called because of its medial location among five regions—Thuringia, Franconia, Buchen, Hesse, and the Eichsfeld. This elevation had formerly been the site of Herr von Franckenstein's castle, built in 455 A.D. The reader is reminded that the Wartburg did not yet exist at that time and was subsequently destroyed in 1259 A.D. The omission of the year of the actual construction points to Limberg's *modus operandi* and his dubious reliability as a chronicler. Sufficiently intrigued by the legend surrounding the hill, the narrator undertakes climbing it. Having appraised the hilltop as a piece of real estate of doubtful value, he begins with the central plot, the legend: "Von diesem Berge erzehlet man gar artige Sachen / wie nemlich einsmahls ein Münch eine Nonne lange Zeit caressirt / sie zu seinem Willen zu bringen / wirfft ihr in der Kirchen offters viel tausend blinde Küsse zu / (wie solches auch noch heutiges Tages Münch und Nonne im Gebrauch haben)" (Limberg, p. 275). Questionable mores, a condition persisting in the monastic establishments of his time, are passed off by Limberg as a matter of common knowledge. Beyond that, he is grossly unkind in his portrayal of the young monk and nun who were punished for their "perfidy" through instant petrifaction. The narrative lacks subtlety of touch and development. The lascivious monk "...redet sie [die Nonne] mit gar süssen Worten an / kan sie aber zu seinen Willen nicht bringen sondern sagt / wenn ich das thue / mögen wir beyde wohl zu Steinen werden" (Limberg, p. 275). There is no indication of the time span involved in the unfortunate courtship. Crudely, it is a tangible object—a bottle of rare wine and presumably its effect—that induces the stimulus which persuades the nun to meet the monk on the mountain: "...da läst sie sich überreden / und gehen miteinander auf diesen Berg / und küssen einander so lange / daß die Mäuler an einander gewachsen..." (Limberg, p. 275). Limberg continues indulging in descriptive metaphor of questionable taste, and goes out of his way to involve other members of the monastic community: the prior, who surprises the two in broad daylight, lectures the monk for his infamy, and tries to guard the innocence of the nun; a lay brother is dispatched to fetch the prior back; a fat monk—presumably the cook, and a thin monk, in all likelihood the cellarer. In the tradition of primitive literature, the original favors readily observable basic traits—physical and moral—over more demanding processes, so as to heighten its popular appeal to the less sophisticated. The Limberg source expounds this aspect in such references as "...ein dicker Noll-Bruder.../ ist vielleicht der Koch..." or "...ein langer / schmaler / margerer [sic] Münch (ist villeicht der Keller-Meister / dann die Keller in den Klöstern sind gemeiniglich tieff/)" (Limberg, p. 277). The narrator confuses the reader by awkwardly intermingling description of the scene and the action itself. He obviously becomes so steeped in his censure of the institution which the monk and the nun represent that he fails to report the actual event of their punishment—the petrification, be it from zeal or lack of acumen. Limberg closes the frame around his narration with a reference to the episode as an amusing, if unlikely *Curiosität*, and an invitation to any doubting reader to follow his, the narrator's, example—that is, to climb the hill and behold the scene himself.

1775, the year of publication of *Der Mönch und die Nonne auf dem Mittelstein* marks the beginning of a new period in

Wieland's verse narratives—a period which may be regarded as starting point of his *humoristische Klassik* (ca. 1774-1783), Sengle advises (Sengle, pp. 344-345). Here one finds an objectivity and a depth not hitherto present in Wieland's Rococo epic, a quality which bespeaks his growing maturity and his conquest of the excesses of *Schwärmerei* and frivolity. At that time, the spirit of *Empfindsamkeit* appears to have been lingering still at the court of Weimar. In the same year, 1775, Wieland—by request of the Duchess Anna Amalia— made the painful, hopeless love of a young nun the subject of a sentimental cantata, entitled *Seraphina*. Other than certain plot elements, this product bears little resemblance to the atmosphere prevailing in *Der Mönch und die Nonne auf dem Mittelstein*. The latter is free from considerations of ducal wishes and sentiments in motif and tone. As editor of *Der Teutsche Merkur* (1773-1810) Wieland was keenly aware of the current literary trend and the growing penchant for *Volkstümlichkeit*. It is surely no coincidence that fairy and legendary themes—mostly foreign—constitute the plots of most of Wieland's verse narratives in which he reached the acme of his artistic niveau between 1774 and 1783. Yet, Wieland who never completely embraced any literary movement was too much the enlightened skeptic and the poetic craftsman as to feel at home in a genuine *Sturm und Drang* situation or to condone its rashness. It is, indeed, inconceivable that he would ever produce true "folk" literature which in its naiveté was essentially incompatible with his subtlety and cosmopolitanism. Wieland's choice of the tale under consideration might be viewed as a concession to the *Sturm und Drang*—a gesture to meet the demands of the younger generation—and a challenge to refashion and embellish an inferior literary product. One may observe a similar intention in certain aspects of *Das Wintermährchen* (1776), *Der Vogelsang oder die drei Lehren* (1778), and *Pervonte oder die Wünsche* (1779).

Wieland took to task monastic asceticism on other occasions.[5] While his version of the legend is an articulate testimonial to his rejection of monasticism, of philistinism, and, in general, of hypocrisy, his censure of an illicit relationship within a monastic community is secondary to the commiseration with the two young people and their adversity. As Sengle observes, "Es geht hier nicht um den Mönch und die Nonne als solche, sondern um das allgemein-menschliche Schicksal eines Liebespaares, dem... eine legitime Vereinigung verwehrt ist. Darum wurde wohl auch später der weniger mißverständliche Titel 'Sixt und Clärchen' gewählt" (Sengle, p. 345).

Following the prose preface relative to his source, Wieland begins the actual verse narrative with a *Prolog* humorously reflecting on the negligible value of the monastic vocation. The vow itself which deprives a member of every mundane comfort, and obligates him for life "bey wohlverschloßnen Thüren / Zu fasten und zu psalmodiren" (*T.M.*, III, 195), elicits Wieland's awe as a "Wagstück" commanding profound conviction. It is this very quality which the hero and heroine of the narrative are lacking. At the end of the prologue, Wieland hints at the forthcoming "lesson" while providing a frame for the actual plot and defending the value of the inconspicuous genre of the fairy tale:

> Ergötzt es euch, so hat der Dichter halb erreicht,
> Was er dem Leser gerne gönnte;
> Denn, glaubet mir, kein Mährchen ist so seicht,
> Aus dem ein Mann nicht weiser werden könnte
> (*T.M.*, III, 195).

In the opening lines of Canto I, the exposition, as it were, both Wieland's doggerel-clad irony and a manifestation of the sequestered pair's inexperienced youth are apparent from the repeated diminutives:

> Ein frommes klösterliches Pärchen,
> Er, Bruder Sixt, Sie, Schwester, Clärchen,
> Noch beyde jung und schön und zart
> Und fromm und gut nach teutscher Art
> (*T.M.*, III, 196).

The poor, unsuspecting souls fall prey to the "...süsse

Gift der Liebe..." (*T.M.*, III, 197). As in most other instances involving this emotion, Wieland does not preach or condemn. He merely warns of the consequences sure to ensue from an act branded as "sinful" by the moral codes of church and society alike. The poet—much to the chagrin of some of his critics— makes his own position clear when he speaks of the pair's lamentable situation, and of Sixt's ambitious inclination:

> In meinen Augen, daß ihrs wißt,
> Macht Sixten diese Schwachheit Ehre.
> Ein Mensch, der doch kein Engel ist,
> Kann traun! um kleinern Sold nicht minnen!
> (*T.M.*, III, 199).

Sixt and Clärchen experience all the nuances of passion: from the "dunkle nahmenlose Sehnen..." "...zum stumpfen Schmerz" (*T.M.*, III, 197). Yet,

> Ihr Schmerz ist ein zu süsser Schmerz,
> Als daß man gleich an Heilung dächte
> (*T.M.*, III, 200);

and they reject the duty and comfort of confession for fear of ending their joys and hopes—however faint—of togetherness.

While the original makes no mention of the time element involved in the development of the relationship, Wieland heightens the dramatic impact of his version by means of a slowly rising curve of action. The pair's mutual fixation secretly dominates every aspect of its monastic life and duty, including meditation. Three years of prayers and mortification fail to sublimate the passion.

In place of the bottle of wine which stimulates the secret meeting in the Limberg source, Wieland refined the crude motivation of his model by employing the device of the dream in Canto II of his poem. A thrice repeated dream vision arranged by a protective spirit serves not only as a promise of fulfillment, but also as an omen for guidance to which especially Clärchen clings. Her timid "Nie hätt' ich's aus mir selbst gewagt!" (*T.M.*, IV, 12) reveals the degree of her dependence upon the supernatural phenomenon. Indeed, this welcome extraneous influence provides the impetus for her ultimate rendezvous with Sixt. No matter what the measure of rationalization and the moral implications in this convenient shift of blame or responsibility may be, Wieland achieved artistic effect through this device without sacrificing the genuinely human sentiment which pervades his work. Still plagued by misgivings—an impediment hardly considered in the original legend—the two nevertheless yield to the omen. Wieland contrived their escape at Easter time, thus compounding the gravity of the sacrilege for the purpose of impact.

In contrast to his model, Wieland concentrated solely on the two principal characters. When the two lovers meet at last, his version practices conscious discretion. Compared with the crudities of his model, Wieland's apparent, widely censured frivolity exudes aesthetic refinement.

Although Wieland paralleled his model in the resolution— the pair's petrifaction—he was far from echoing the "just deserts" conclusion. Instead, his liberal spirit went so far as to involve Heaven, surely an undue reward and a glorification of love, be it "pure" or otherwise.

> Ich seh, ich seh sie, Brust an Brust,
> Entseelt von grenzenloser Lust
> Die Augen starr gen Himmel heben;
> Er hat sich aufgethan, sie schweben
> In seinem Wonneglanz daher,
> Nichts sterblichs ist an ihnen mehr,
> Sie schweben auf ins ew'ge Leben
> (*T.M.*, IV, 14).

These words evidently allude to the pair's boundless bliss. Eight additional lines following the passage just cited concluded Canto II in the original *T.M.* version. At the same time, they seem to have been intended as a transition to the anticipated third Canto which presumably was to have elaborated on the manner of the couple's suffering after death.

> Glückselige, in euerm Wahn,
> (Wofern Empfindung Wahn zu nennen
> Erlaubt ist) labet euch daran,
> So lagn [sic] es Lieb und Schicksal gönnen!
> Es ist ein Traum, ein Augenblick!
> Ihr habt ihn wohl verdienen müssen,
> Und werdet für ein kurzes Glück
> Zu bald nur und zu lange büßen
> (*T.M.*, IV, 15).

To be sure, the third Canto never materialized. Instead, Wieland later undertook to modify the conclusion of the poem by omitting the eight lines cited above and replacing them with the following:

> Versteinert bleibt ihr Leib zurück,
> Und zeigt, noch warm vom heil'gen Triebe,
> Des Wandrers sanft gerührtem Blick
> Dieß ew'ge Denkmal ihrer Liebe
> (XXI, 40).

Wieland's motives for the change remain open to speculation. Be it his realization that the event of the pair's ultimate unification in this life sufficiently engaged the reader's sympathy to end the narrative, or the result of mature, aesthetic deliberation—the method enhanced the appeal. Klee whose inquiry is limited to the identification of Wieland's source and the intricacies surrounding the two versions of the conclusion, conceives of the mode of revision—its economy and effect—as a rare *tour de force*. While the lovers' earthly felicity and death coincide, their continued blissful companionship in the hereafter is virtually assured. Wieland displays his proverbial *Diesseitsfreudigkeit* by removing the threat of further atonement after having duly paid for their transgression on earth. In creating a lasting monument to the love of two individuals which his source had maliciously condemned, Wieland successfully culminated his travesty. Clearly, he was more concerned with aesthetic than with moral aspects. His attitude was alien to a consistent, heavy didacticism, even though a dose of censure and warning is an inherent part of his subtle belletristic moralizing.

In his *Sixt und Clärchen* the enlightened satirist blended delicate irony and humorous skepticism with a diction which elevates spirit and tone of the crude legend that served as his model. Rather than encountering merely a comical parody or a burlesque imitation, the reader is acutely aware that a conscious craftsman was at work here.

4

THE FABLE

The year 1778 marked the completion of one of Wieland's most simple, naive, and didactic verse narratives—probably the tamest of his travesties, one that almost defies characterization. *Der Vogelsang oder die drei Lehren* was adapted from *Lays de l'Oiselet* in Pierre Jean Baptiste Legrand d'Aussy's *Fabliaux ou Contes du douzième et du treizième Siècle*, I, based on a collection of 1765, according to Gruber.

Wieland had called on a *fabliau* before to serve as a model. In 1777 he had undertaken his poetic version of *La Mule sans Frein*, *Das Sommermährchen*, an infinitely more farcical adaptation than *Der Vogelsang*. While animals have played a part elsewhere in Wieland's work, *Der Vogelsang* is the only narrative involving a reasoning, acting, and talking animal, as does its model. I therefore felt justified in treating it under a separate subheading, particularly since the fable is widely associated with the *Aufklärung* as its most prominent, favorite literary genre. Although Wieland never ignored the "storehouse" of nature as a source of inspiration, and had, on occasion, drawn from it liberally, he manifested little interest in the genuine fable.

Wieland conceived of the fable as the oldest pedagogic device, and of the allegory as an ancient suggestion of philosophy. In the preface to the first part of the *Dschinnistan* collection the poet reminds the reader that the history of mankind commences with narratives involving talking animals and theophanies. Yet, the more or less soberly moralizing animal fable which bears utterly upon its lesson found little favor with Wieland.

The *fabliau*, commonly defined as a short, comical, often coarse verse narrative prominent in the twelfth and thirteenth centuries is likely to have engaged Wieland's imagination to a greater degree. It was sure to foster his preoccupation with the past while satisfying his fascination with ironically colored, eccentric themes. Indeed, he chose *fabliaux* as models on two other occasions (*cf. Das Sommermährchen*, and *Die Wasserkufe*). Right or wrong, Gruber cited Wieland's source of *Der Vogelsang* as a *fabliau*. To be sure, the poet actually modeled his verse adaptation after prose versions of the original *fabliau*—renderings which in all probability had undergone some refinement to conform to the standards of eighteenth-century propriety.

Contrasted with his source, Wieland seems to have given in to an impulse of rare *Deutschtümelei*, perhaps for the purpose of appealing more directly to his compatriots. Sengle suspects in this manifestation possibly "eine humorvolle Selbstrechtfertigung gegenüber dem Hof, von dem sich der Dichter... immer weiter entfernt...," and "...eine persönliche Note..." (Sengle, pp. 356-357).

The action takes place "...in meinem Schwabenland" (XXII, 69), the hero—or rather, the villain—is simply Hans, a wealthy, cunning individual of dubious background. His character, and his domicile—a splendid palace—are patterned after his source. Wieland, however, achieved superior artistic effect by hinting at both Hans's character and the magic element, mainly by means of the dash and the insertion:

> Vor ungefähr fünf hundert Jahren
> Und drüber, lebt' in meinem Schwabenland
> Ein reicher Erdensohn, von Namen unbekannt,
> (Weil seine Ahnen stets geheim geblieben waren)
> und drum kurzweg der reiche Hans genannt.

> Von Gottes Gnaden hatte der
> Ein schönes Schloß,—das bessern einst als er
> Zum Aufenthalt gedient—man weiß nicht wie,
>   gewonnen   (XXII, 69).

Wieland enlarged upon the intent of the model to concentrate a whole register of vices—indolence, stupidity, avarice, inordinate curiosity—in the human character as the negative element while investing the animal, the little magic bird, with desirable human traits. Yet, his elaborations do not rest solely on any of these factors. He retained the medieval spirit of his source in tender nuances, as well, particularly in the charming simplicity of the bird's articulate songs. Significantly, Wieland's verse expands on the prose version in a passage announcing the forthcoming "lesson" addressed to the assembled audience. The primitive plot develops by means of a fable-like dialogue between man and bird. The greedy squire who decides to catch and sell the marvelous bird for a high price compounds his threats while the bird that cannot sing in captivity continues to plead for its life. Ultimately, bird succeeds in outwitting man by appealing to one of the latter's cardinal weaknesses: his morbid curiosity about three "wonderful," profitable precepts on the condition that the bird is let free. From a safe spot the bird then dispenses the didactic compendium of human prudence in three commands which is identical in Wieland's source and his own version: first, do not be gullible; secondly, do not cry over what you have never had; thirdly, once you have it, never let it go. Wieland's bird continues to tax the vexation of the desperate Hans by pretending to have a magic stone of inestimable powers in his stomach, until he convinces the greedy dullard of this improbability. The wonderful bird flies away and with it the life and beauty of the estate are gone.

The elements of travesty are scant in this narrative which parallels its source and its spirit rather closely. One may observe some broadening, however. Wieland's departure from his usual pattern of universally colored characters in regions of exotic or merely general description is uncommon. Relating plot and scene to his own home, Swabia, imposes geographic limitations, as it were, and renders his criticism more pointed, yet also less cosmopolitan. On the one hand, he clearly strives for *Volkstümlichkeit* by sprinkling his narrative with popular proverbs and figures of speech. On the other hand, I have cited understatement as one of his sophisticated poetic devices in dealing with the leading character.

In spite of the popular veneer which Wieland applied in this adaptation his gentle travesty lies probably in the resolution. While his source—true to the tradition of the fable—neatly sums up the didactic message so as to leave no chance of doubt about its intention, Wieland prefers to imply it. He refrains from belaboring the obvious. Instead, he crisply presents to the reader the consequences of the vices exhibited here: "Weg ist das ganze Feenland, / Und ihm bleibt nichts als dürrer Sand" (XXII, 86). Again, the fantastic element which is, to some degree, also common to some fables, serves the poet's purpose. In recasting the original fable he manifested the same restraint and humorous reservation toward his characters that has been observed in regard to the fairy tale. The master's touch consists in altering the ponderous morale of his model's conclusion to a brisk, facetious *fait accompli*.

CONCLUSION

If critics and literary historians have long maintained that Wieland's merits have been underrated, the frequent lament should have specific application to the area of the travesty. As evidenced in the past chapters, Wieland's efforts toward aesthetic refinement of a hitherto questionable genre should contribute materially to the revaluation of his stature, as well as to the justification of the travesty as a legitimate literary product.

Of course, Wieland incurred a debt to numerable sources—mostly foreign—but the travesty by definition involves the existence of a model. Viewed in this light, one cannot but refute the protagonists of a position who inveigh against his plagiaristic machinations. The issue of originality presents a fundamental problem in literature. René Wellek points out that "Originality is usually misconceived in our time as meaning a mere violation of tradition, or it is sought for at the wrong place, in the mere material of the work of art, or in its mere scaffolding—the traditional plot, the conventional framework... recurrent themes and images which were handed down from antiquity through the Latin Middle Ages... permeate all modern literatures. No author felt inferior or unoriginal because he used, adapted, and modified themes and images inherited from tradition and sanctioned by antiquity."[1] Wieland made no secret of his tendency to borrow plots from other sources, indeed, he humbly admitted his negligible power of imagination (cf. L, 126). Moreover, he properly acknowledged his sources, and he did them credit through his aesthetic treatment.

Although Wieland made no specific point of creating travesties, his choice of sources for adaptation reflects his discretion and sensitivity to the *dulce*, the *utile*, or both, in literature. The question why he did not attach the label "travesty" to his products in the parodistic genre suggests various possibilities which are open to argument: either he was too much on the defensive about the "imitative" nature of some of his works to call further attention to this much censured quality; or he felt that there was no need to belabor the obvious; or, more likely, he did not want to be associated with the travesty which up to that point had been tinged by an aura of disrepute. At any rate, in Wieland's case the travesty assumes the character of a defense mechanism. To all appearances, he was unaware of his actual, prominent contribution to an underdeveloped facet of German literature—a contribution which only in retrospect has been recognized as worthwhile. One of his rare appraisals of the satirical genre and some of its attending possibilities and problems is contained in a letter to Blumauer, dated September 25, 1788, on the occasion of the latter's *Aeneis* (Vol. II, 1782; other vols., including Vol. IX, 1788):

> Ich bin meiner individuellen Gesinnungsart nach sonst eben kein besonderer Freund der burlesken Dichtart. Aber der Gedanke, die Äneis auf eine solche Art und nach einem solchen Plan zu travestiren, daß Sie dadurch Gelegenheit bekommen, auf eine indirekte Art, lachend und zu lachen machend, eine der größten und gemeinnützlichsten Absichten Ihres großen Monarchen zu befördern, dieser Gedanke ist Ihnen von einem Gott eingegeben worden.... Wenige wissen vielleicht, wie schwer es ist, und wie viel dazu gehört, ein poetisches Abentheuer, wie dieses ist, mit Ehre zu bestehen, und wie sehr ein solches Werk bey aller anscheinenden Leichtigkeit,...die schärfste Probe über den Verstand und Geschmack eines Dichters ist (*DB*, II, 85).

Wieland displayed remarkable versatility. He called on the more demanding genres, such as the novel, and the epic, to serve as models—wholly or partially—for his adaptations. Findings reveal, however, that he seems to have preferred the less exalted genres for this purpose (*cf.* Chapter IV); indeed, volume and quality of the production indicate that he was more at home with the humbler sources, an overwhelming majority of which was narratives in the fantastic vein. While elements of the travesty are present in his adaptations from the novels and epics, there are no pure travesties in these categories. His preoccupation with nature and the supernatural is another striking feature in his adaptations and certainly a rare element in the realm of parodistic literature.

By inclination and as a child of his age, Wieland had a didactic tendency. I have shown his preference for motifs—however colorful the frame—which afford an opportunity for gentle moralizing. In the travesty he used the hortatory element to good advantage, subtly and generally with an admixture of delicate humor and irony which invariably coated the message.

The factor which perhaps more than any other constitutes Wieland's merit for modernizing the travesty in German literature is his ability to depersonalize, and thereby to achieve more universally valid results from his message. Rather than overtly attacking or ridiculing the author of his source in a demonstrative gesture of "doing better" he was prone to take to task the work as a whole or in part. Even more often, he has been shown to parody certain literary genres, *e.g.*, the traditional epic, or the crude folk tale, especially works without a known author. The poet eloquently demonstrated his skill in the artful reduction of the sublime without carrying the enterprise to the ridiculous—a manifestation more of antiidolatry than of blasphemy. The temperate emotional climate which his parodistic products eventually assumed endows them with an amiable quality. His travesties widely mirror his attitude toward matters exalted: he did not take them seriously, without taking them in vain. His gentle scorn extended to society, to accepted systems of politics and religion, to the realms of education and literature, and their representatives.

The treatment of his characters is generally humane. Wieland felt no need for reducing them to caricatures by distorting their physical features. Instead, a subtle twist to their mental or moral makeup accomplished the desired transformation. More than any other segment of society Wieland seems to have singled out the image of the absolute monarch, and the hierarchy of the church for his most berating characterizations. The potentate—probably the best though invariably negative of his three-dimensional character portrayals—almost attains the proportion of a prototype.

Far more extensively than with any individuals or institution, Wieland dealt with intangible—spiritual and moral—attributes, or the lack of them. In his humorous, pseudophilosophical reflections on the subject of virtue he questioned nature and substance of this most idealized abstraction in the Age of the Enlightenment. His witty skepticism was on guard against assorted vices such as narrow-minded provincialism, false pretense, popular inhibitions, social taboos, prudishness, philistinism, and above all, hypocrisy. Wieland succeeded in isolating these shortcomings and taking them to task articulately in his adaptations. In the tradition of the foremost *cognesci* of the human psyche, Wieland brought psychological insight and deepening to the travesty, a notable addendum to a traditionally fairly insensitive genre. This exceptional flair, especially in crucial moments, was instrumental in modulating the mood, and not rarely the resolution, by convincingly involving his characters' emotions. He was out to humanize the figures of his models—mortals and fantastic creatures alike—and he admirably invested each character with three dimensions. The spirit of *humanitas* extends beyond his remodeled characters, it gently deemphasizes venerated ideals and institutions; it seeks to secularize them, one might say.

Some of Wieland's travesties represent a poetic social experiment; almost all of them are a protest against puritanism, whatever the form. The lack of precision for which Wieland was often criticized behooves his method in the travesty. Whether calculated or unintentionally achieved, an absence of sharp delineation enhances the mood and tends to temper the satirical element. The result is a more "civil," mellowed product than the travesty had been known to be up to Wieland's time.

A vast majority of Wieland's travesties resulted from adaptations of prose models into carefully wrought verse narratives. In general, the poet's consistent tendency toward economy in plot development is evident. His attention to discriminating rhetorical practices is a rarity in the area of the travesty which may not have been considered worthy of painstaking detail and aesthetic reflection. By a caprice of punctuation—a mere dash, for example—he knew how to heighten the suspense, retard the action, or reverse the denouement. His diction, a spectrum of fine nuances, is capable of being energetic, tantalizing, or pensive, but not venomous or coarse even when it gives voice to censure or warning. His finesse in adapting motifs of questionable taste manifests rare skill in the gallant tradition of discreetly indicating and hinting at that which had preferably remain unsaid.

No matter what the plot might be, Wieland imbued his adaptations with dignity, and succeeded in raising the artistic niveau of the travesty. By skillful manipulation of psychological processes he managed to deepen the issues with uncommon delicacy, and to modernize the concept of the old, perfunctory travesty—indeed a somewhat problematic genre which thrived on distortion of its models and capitalized on sensational or lewd aspects.

The quality of triviality which was often, if unfairly, ascribed to Wieland's work, to products of the Rococo, and certainly to the travesty as a negligible genre, seems to suggest a kinship to Bouhour's (1628-1702) principle of *délicatesse* which seeks to foster the art of indirection.[2] Ernst Cassirer elaborates on the danger of aesthetic triviality which can be avoided "...nur durch die Art der Einführung und der Einkleidung des Gedankens, durch irgendeine überraschende Wendung im A̱ṵs̱ḏṟu c k desselben..." (Cassirer, p. 403). Truth or precision alone does not lend artistic justification to a creation, according to the ideal of Bouhour. The illusion of ambiguity (the *équivoque*), when coupled with truth to form an aesthetic entity, becomes defensible and, in fact, desirable as a safeguard against triviality (Cassirer, p. 403). Certainly, Wieland satisfied the aesthetic demand of emphasizing the expression rather than the content of the thought. Wieland's travesties exude agility and resourcefulness through his grasp of nuances and rapid transition of meaning. The utilization of the *je ne sais quoi* and its ramifications, beyond the limitations of a charming stock phrase, is a sensitive device which involves indirect knowledge. As a delicate challenge it hints and teases where the older parodistic tradition may have accused, scorned or laughed. The degree to which Wieland cultivated the intangible, uncertain quality of the "I know not what" indicates an intentional exercise of a rhetorical device rather than a poetic shortcoming. This lack of plasticity represents a vitalizing influence in his adaptations.

In relationship to his work as a whole, Wieland's travesties constitute indeed an impressive portion of his literary production. Peculiarly, the peak period of his artistic maturity coincides with the height of his accomplishments—in terms of both quantity and quality—in the area of the travesty. The same discriminating workmanship which marks his more demanding products prevails in his adroit, parodistic writings. Whatever slighting effect was intended in these adaptations was achieved through thoughtful manipulation of a blend of sound ideas and aesthetic refinement.

Wieland's travesty or its elements may be considered a pioneering effort in the development of modern parodistic literature of the highest artistic niveau. To be sure, it is doubtful that Wieland's virtuosity and fastidiousness in his verse adaptations were attempted, let alone equaled, in subsequent travesties, even though the institution of the verse narrative did not become unfashionable for some time. Aside from the trends which Wieland set in his travesties, they mark a curious projection of his poetic powers. These good-natured products of a seasoned, witty, skeptical rationalist command our regard as reflecting the ideal of balance and harmony of the author, as well as of the age in which they originated.

Moreover, German literature is—or should be—indebted to Wieland for deepening and legitimizing the niche of the travesty as a genre.

NOTES

NOTES TO INTRODUCTION

[1] Friedrich Sengle, *Wieland* (Stuttgart, 1949), p. 9. This source is cited hereafter as Sengle.
[2] *C. M. Wielands sämmtliche Werke*, ed. J. G. Gruber, Vol. L of 53 vols. (Leipzig: Göschen, 1824-1828), 126. This edition is the source of the original Wieland texts to be quoted in this study. Other sources will be documented when cited.
[3] Friedrich Beißner, Emil Staiger, Friedrich Sengle, Hans Werner Seiffert, *Wieland*. Vier Bieberacher Vorträge 1953 (Wiesbaden, 1954), p. 33.
[4] *The Oxford English Dictionary*, XI (Oxford, 1933), 297, defines "travesty" in the etymological sense as "An alteration of dress or appearance; a disguise," and as "A literary composition which aims at exciting laughter by burlesque or ludicrous treatment of a serious work...."
[5] Ferdinand Josef Schneider, *Die deutsche Dichtung der Aufklärungszeit* (Stuttgart, 1948), p. 283. Hereafter cited as Schneider.

NOTES TO CHAPTER I

[1] Werner P. Friederich, *Dante's Fame Abroad. 1350-1850* (Chapel Hill' 1950), p. 371.
[2] Bärbel B. Cantarino, "Aloys Blumauer and the Literature of Austrian Enlightenment" (diss. University of North Carolina, 1967), pp. 119, 135.
[3] Erwin Frank Ritter, "Johann Baptist von Alxinger. A Literary Profile of the Austrian Enlightenment" (diss. University of North Carolina, 1967), p. 26.
[4] *Goethes Werke*, ed. Wolfgang Kayser, IV (Hamburg, 1953, 1960), 537-538.

NOTES TO CHAPTER II

1. Emil Ermatinger, *Deutsche Dichtung 1750-1900* (Frankfurt am Main, Bonn, 1961), p. 172. Hereafter cited as Ermatinger.
2. Ludwig Hirzel, *Wielands Beziehungen zu den deutschen Romantikern* (Bern, 1904), p. 70.
3. Gotthold Ephraim Lessing, *Sämmtliche Schriften*, ed. Karl Lachmann, VI (Leipzig, 1854), 17.
4. *Ibid.*, 29.
5. I. S. Stamm, "Wieland and Sceptical Rationalism," *The Germanic Review*, XXXIII, No. 1 (February 1958), 28-29.
6. Ermatinger, pp. 38-39.
7. Christoph Martin Wieland, *Auswahl denkwürdiger Briefe von C. M. Wieland*, ed. Ludwig Wieland, I (Wien, 1815), 6-7. Hereafter cited as *DB*.
8. Ferdinand Josef Schneider, *Die deutsche Dichtung vom Ausgang des Barocks bis zum Beginn des Klassizismus 1700-1785* (Stuttgart, 1924), p. 237. Cited as Schneider, *Barock-Klassizismus*.
9. Johann Heinrich Merck, *Schriften und Briefwechsel*, ed. K. Wolff, II (Leipzig, 1909), 100.
10. Christoph Martin Wieland, *Wieland's Werke*, XXX (Berlin, n.d.), 6. This source is cited as Wieland.
11. Friedrich Sengle, "Von Wielands Epenfragmenten zum 'Oberon,'" *Arbeiten zur deutschen Literatur 1750-1850* (Stuttgart, 1965), p. 58. Hereafter cited as Sengle, *Arbeiten*.

NOTES TO CHAPTER III

1. Victor Michel, *C. M. Wieland, La Formation et l'évolution de son esprit jusqu'en 1772, Etudes de littérature étrangère et comparée*, 10 (Paris, n. d.), pp. 63 f. Hereafter cited as Michel.
2. Christoph Martin Wieland, *Ausgewählte Briefe von C. M. Wieland an verschiedene Freunde in den Jahren 1751. bis 1810. geschrieben, und nach der Zeitfolge geordnet*, Vol. II of 4 vols. (Zürich, 1815), 330. This collection is hereafter cited as *AB*.
3. *Cf.* Christoph Martin Wieland, "Die Abderiten. An den Leser," *Der Teutsche Merkur* (hereafter cited as *T.M.*), III (July 1778), 26-59; (August 1778), 129-144; (September 1778), 218-240; IV (October 1778), 37-46; (November 1778), 117-136.
4. To be cited as *Bibliothèque*.
5. This version was contained in the *Bibliothèque Universelle des Romans*, II (Paris, April 1778), 7 ff.
6. Anne Louise Germaine de Staël-Holstein, *De l'Allemagne* (Paris, 1883), p. 173.
7. Max Koch, *Das Quellenverhältniß von Wielands Oberon* (Marburg, 1880), p. 4. Hereafter cited as Koch.

⁸ Richard Newald, *Geschichte der deutschen Literatur von den Anfängen bis zur Gegenwart*. VI, I: *Von Klopstock bis zu Goethes Tod* (München, 1961), 97.

NOTES TO CHAPTER IV
1. THE SHORT MIXED NARRATIVE
¹ John Milton, *Paradise Lost* (London, 1719), pp. 93-94.
² P. Ovidius Naso, *Metamorphoses*, ed. Rudolf Ehwald, VII (Leipzig, 1925), pp. 148 ff.
³ The references are to Ariosto's *Orlando Furioso*, Cantos XLII-XLIII, and to La Fontaine's *La Coupe Enchantée* in the *Contes et Nouvelles* (*cf.* VII, 237).
⁴ Lukian, *Sämtliche Werke*, trans. C. M. Wieland, ed. Hanns Floerke, IV (München, Leipzig, 1911). Hereafter cited as Lukian.

2. THE FAIRY TALE
¹ *Les Mille et Une Nuits, Contes Arabes*, trans. Antoine Galland, I (Paris, 1818), 184.
² *Ibid.*, 120.

3. THE LEGEND
¹ The poem appeared originally with this title in *Der Teutsche Merkur*, III (March 1775), 193-205 and IV (April 1775), 3-15. Hereafter cited in the text as *T.M.* Later Wieland adopted the title *Sixt und Clärchen oder der Mönch und die Nonne auf dem Mädelstein* (a variant of *Mittelstein*).
² Gotthold Klee, "Wielands Gedicht 'Sixt und Klärchen,' sein ursprünglicher Plan und seine Quelle," *Zeitschrift für den deutschen Unterricht*, XIII, xi (1899), 728-730. Hereafter cited as Klee.
³ *Das im Jahr 1708. lebende und schwebende Eisenach*, ed. Johann Limberg (Eisenach, 1712). The Limberg text was released to me only recently in microfilm by permission of the *Staatliche Archivverwaltung, Ministerium des Innern*, through *Thüringisches Landeshauptarchiv*, Weimar. Quotations from this text will be cited as Limberg.
⁴ Wilhelm Kosch, *Deutsches Literatur-Lexikon*, II (Bern, 1953), 1536.
⁵ *Cf, e.g.*, the biting *Briefe über das Mönchswesen* (1771) which, to be sure, are credited chiefly to Georg Michael La Roche. *Cf.* also, *Der goldne Spiegel* (1772), *Die Wasserkufe* (1795).

NOTES TO CONCLUSION

[1] René Wellek and Austin Warren, *Theory of Literature* (New York, 1956), p. 249.
[2] Ernst Cassirer, *Die Philosophie der Aufklärung* (Tübingen, 1932), p. 403. Hereafter cited as Cassirer.

BIBLIOGRAPHY

I. WIELAND'S COLLECTED WORKS AND LETTERS

WIELAND, CHRISTOPH MARTIN. *Ausgewählte Briefe an verschiedene Freunde in den Jahren 1751. bis 1810. geschrieben, und nach der Zeitfolge geordnet.* Vols. II, IV. Zürich, 1815.
— *Ausgewählte Werke in drei Bänden,* ed. Friedrich Beißner. München, 1964.
— *Auswahl denkwürdiger Briefe,* ed. Ludwig Wieland. Vols. I, II. Wien, 1815.
— *Dschinnistan oder Auserlesene Feen- und Geistermärchen,* ed. Albert Ehrenstein. Leipzig, 1922.
— *Neue Briefe vornehmlich an Sophie von La Roche,* ed. Robert Hassencamp. Stuttgart, 1894.
— *Sämmtliche Werke,* ed. J. G. Gruber. 53 vols. Leipzig: Göschen, 1824-1828.
— et al., ed. *Der Teutsche Merkur.* Weimar, 1773-1810.
— *Werke,* ed. H. Düntzer. Vol. XXX. Berlin, n.d. [1879 f.].
— *Werke,* ed. Gotthold Klee. 4 vols. Leipzig, Wien, n.d. [1900].
— *Werke,* eds. Fritz Martini and Hans Werner Seiffert. 5 vols. München, 1964-1968.

II. OTHER PRIMARY SOURCES

ADDISON, JOSEPH. *The Works,* ed. George Washington Greene. 6 vols. Philadelphia, 1876.
Amadis de Gaula, ed. Vasco Lobeira, trans. Robert Southey from the Spanish version of García Ordóñez de Montalvo. London, 1872.
Amadis de Gaula, trans. Nicolas de Herberay. Paris, 1560.
ANSTEY, CHRISTOPHER. *The New Bath Guide or Memoirs of the B-N-R-D Family.* London, 1788.
ARIOSTO, LUDOVICO. *The Orlando furioso,* trans. William Stewart Rose. 2 vols. London, 1907-1910.
BAR, BARON GEORG LUDWIG VON. *Epîtres diverses sur des Sujets différents.* London, 1740.

BERGENELSEN, JOHANN VON. *Das im Jahr 1708 lebende und schwebende Eisenach.* Stralsund, 1709.
Bibliothèque Universelle des Romans, ed. A. R. Voyer d'Argenson et al. Vols. II (January 1776), I (October 1776), (September 1777), I (October 1777), II (April 1778), II (July 1780). Paris, 1775-1789.
BLUMAUER, ALOYS. *Virgil's Aeneis travestirt* (1784-1788), ed. Eduard Grisebach. Leipzig, 1872.
BOCCACCIO, GIOVANNI. *The Decameron*, trans. Richard Aldington. London, 1857.
BODMER, JOHANN JAKOB. *Polytimet.* Zürich, 1760.
BOUHOURS, DOMINIQUE. *Les Entretiens d'Ariste et d'Eugene.* Amsterdam 1671.
BRANT, SEBASTIAN. *Das Narrenschiff* (1494), ed. Karl Goedeke. Leipzig, 1872.
BREITINGER, JOHANN JAKOB. *Critische Dichtkunst* (Faksimiledruck nach der Ausgabe von 1740). Stuttgart, 1966.
Brüggemann, Fritz, ed., *Aus der Frühzeit der deutschen Aufklärung: Christian Thomasius und Christian Weise.* Weimar, Leipzig, 1928.
Le Cabinet des Fées, ou Collection Choisie des Contes des Fées, et autres Contes Merveilleux. Vols. XVI, XI, XX. Amsterdam, Paris, Genève, 1785-1789.
Cervantes Saavedra, Miguel de. *The Ingenious Gentleman Don Quixote de la Mancha*, ed. Samuel Putman. 2 vols. New York, 1958.
CHAUCER, GEOFFREY. *The Canterbury Tales*, ed. Thomas Tyrwhitt. 3 vols. Edinburgh, London, Dublin, 1860.
Claudius, Matthias, ed. *Der Wandsbecker Bothe.* Hamburg, 1771-1775.
De Boor, Helmut, ed. *Das Nibelungenlied.* Wiesbaden, 1957.
DEDEKIND, FRIEDRICH. *Grobianus* (1549), trans. Kaspar Scheidt, ed. Gustav Milchsack. Halle/Saale, 1882.
ERASMUS, DESIDERIUS. *The Praise of Folly* (1508), trans., ed. Hoyt Hopewell Hudson. Princeton, 1941.
FISCHART, JOHANN. *Aller Praktik Großmutter* (1572), ed. Theodor Wilhelm Braune. Halle/Saale, 1876.
— *Geschichtklitterung* (1575), ed. Ute Nyssen (Text der Ausgabe letzter Hand, 1590). 2 vols. Düsseldorf, 1963-1964.
— *Werke*, ed. Adolf Hauffen. 3 vols. Stuttgart, 1892-1895.
Galland, Antoine, trans. *Les Mille et Une Nuits, Contes Arabes.* Vol. I of 7 vols. Paris, 1818.
GERSTENBERG, HEINRICH WILHELM VON. *Ausgewählte Schriften.* Hildburghausen, 1841.
— *Briefe über Merkwürdigkeiten der Litteratur*, ed. A. von Weilen. 2 vols. Heilbronn, 1888-1890.
— *Ugolino* (1768), ed. Christoph Siegrist. Stuttgart, 1966.
Goedeke, Karl, ed. *Schwänke des sechzehnten Jahrhunderts.* Leipzig, 1879.

GOETHE, JOHANN WOLFGANG VON. *Werke*, ed. Wolfgang Kayser, Vols. IV, VI of 14 vols. Hamburg, 1953-1962.
— *Anektode* [sic] *zu den Freuden des jungen Werther*. Leipzig, 1862.
Göttinger Musen-Almanach für 1776-1800, ed. J. H. Voss et al. Hamburg, 1777-1779.
GOTTFRIED VON STRASSBURG. *Tristan und Isolde*, ed. Friedrich Ranke. Berlin, 1958.
GOTTSCHED, JOHANN CHRISTOPH. *Sterbender Cato* (1732), ed. Otto F. Lachmann. Leipzig, 1885.
— *Versuch einer critischen Dichtkunst* (1730). Darmstadt: Wissenschaftliche Buchgesellschaft, 1962.
GRYPHIUS, ANDREAS. *Werke*, ed. Hermann Palm. 2 vols. Berlin, Stuttgart, 1883.
Hagen, Friedrich Heinrich von der, ed. *Minnesinger*. 5 vols. Leipzig, 1838-1861.
HAMILTON, ANTHONY. *Les Quatre Facardins*. Brussels, 1785.
HORATIUS FLACCUS, QUINTUS. *The Complete Works*, ed. Casper J. Kraemer, Jr. New York, 1936..
Huon de Bordeaux, eds. F. Guessard and C. Grandmaison. Paris, 1860.
LA FONTAINE, JEAN DE. *Contes et Nouvelles*. Paris, 1858.
— *Fables*. Paris, n.d.
Legrand d'Aussy, Pierre Jean Baptiste, ed. *Fabliaux ou Contes, Fables et Romans du XIIe et du XIIIe Siècle*. Vols. I, IV, V. Paris, 1829.
LESSING, GOTTHOLD EPHRAIM. *Sämmtliche Schriften*, ed. Karl Lachmann. Vol. VI. Leipzig, 1854.
LIMBERG, JOHANNES. *Denkwürdige Reisebeschreibungen durch Deutschland, Italien, Spanien, Portugal, England, und Schweiz*. (?), 1690.
— ed. *Das im Jahr 1708. lebende und schwebende Eisenach*. Eisenach, 1712.
LUCIANUS SAMOSATENSIS. *Sämtliche Werke*, trans. C. M. Wieland, ed. Hanns Floerke. Vols. II, IV. München, Leipzig, 1911.
LUCRETIUS, CARUS TITUS. *De Rerum Natura*, trans. William Henry Denham Rouse. London, New York, 1924.
MARMONTEL, JEAN FRANÇOIS. *Contes moreaux*. 2 vols. in 1. Paris, 1822.
MERCK, JOHANN HEINRICH. *Schriften und Briefwechsel*, ed. K. Wolff, Vol. II. Leipzig, 1909.
MICHAELIS, JOHANN BENJAMIN. *Sämmtliche Poetische Werke*. Wien, 1794.
MILTON, JOHN. *Comus*, ed. Henry John Todd. Canterbury, 1798.
— *Paradise Lost*. London, 1719.
Müller, Andreas, ed., *Deutsche Literatur in Entwicklungsreihen. Reihe Romantik*. Vol. IX: *Satiren und Parodien*. Leipzig, 1935.
Muncker, Franz, ed., *Anakreontiker und preussisch-patriotische Lyriker*. Stuttgart, 1893-1895.
MURNER, THOMAS. *Die Gäuchmatt* (1515), ed. Wilhelm Uhl. Leipzig, 1879.

— *Die Narrenbeschwörung* (1512), ed. Karl Goedeke. Leipzig, 1879.
— *Schelmenzunft* (1512), ed. Ernst Matthias. Halle/Saale, 1890.
MUSÄUS, JOHANN KARL AUGUST. *Volksmärchen der Deutschen*. 4 vols. Berlin, 1879.
— *Der deutsche Grandison. Auch eine Familiengeschichte* (1778-1779). 2 vols. Eisenach, 1781-1782.
NEUKIRCH, BENJAMIN. *Satyren und Poetische Briefe*. Leipzig, 1732.
NICOLAI, CHRISTOPH FRIEDRICH. *Die Freuden des jungen Werthers. Leiden und Freuden Werthers des Mannes.* Berlin, 1775.
— *Vertraute Briefe von Adelheid B.* an ihre Freundin Julie S.**. Berlin, Stettin, 1799.
OVIDIUS NASO, PUBLIUS. *Metamorphoses*, ed. R. Ehwald. Vol. VII, Leipzig, 1925.
POPE, ALEXANDER. *The Poems*, ed. John Butt. New Haven, 1963.
PRIOR, MATTHEW. *The Poetical Works*. Bell's 2nd ed. Edinburgh, 1784.
RABELAIS, FRANÇOIS. *Oeuvres Complètes*, ed. Jacques Boulenger. Paris, 1955.
ROLLENHAGEN, GEORG. *Der Froschmeuseler* (1595), ed. Karl Goedeke. Leipzig, 1876.
ROST, JOHANN CHRISTOPH. *Versuch von Schäfergedichten und andern poetischen Ausarbeitungen*. Dresden (?), 1756.
SCARRON, PAUL. *Les Oeuvres*. Vols. III, IV, V, VI. Paris, 1668.
SCHLEGEL, JOHANN ELIAS. *Canut* (1746). Copenhagen, 1748.
SHAKESPEARE, WILLIAM. *The Complete Works*, ed. Hardin Craig. New York, 1951.
— *Shakespear Theatralische Werke*, trans. Christoph Martin Wieland. 8 vols. Zürich, 1762-1766.
The Spectator, ed. G. Gregory Smith. 4 vols. London, New York, n.d. [1897-1898].
STAËL-HOLSTEIN DE, ANNE LOUISE GERMAINE. *De l'Allemagne*. Paris, 1883.
Stokes, Francis Griffin, ed. *Epistolae virorum obscurorum*. London, 1925.
STOPPE, DANIEL. *Neue Fabeln oder moralische Gedichte*. Leipzig, 1738, 1740.
TASSO, BERNARDO. *L'Amadigi di Gaula*. Venice, 1836.
TIECK, LUDWIG. *Schriften*. Vol X. Berlin, 1828.
THOMSON, JAMES. *The Seasons*. London, 1792.
VERGILIUS MARO, PUBLIUS. *Aeneid*, trans. C. Day Lewis. New York, 1952.
WECKHERLIN, GEORG RUDOLF. *Gedichte. Bibliothek deutscher Dichter des 17. Jahrhunderts*, ed. W. Müller. Vol. IV. Leipzig, 1823.
WEISE, CHRISTIAN. *Anhang eines neuen Lust-Spiels einer zweyfachen Poetenzunft* (1680). Leipzig, 1683.
WERNHER DER GARTENAERE. *Meier Helmbrecht*, ed. Friedrich Panzer. Halle/Saale, 1930.

WITTENWEILER, HEINRICH. *Der Ring*, ed. Edmund Wiessner. Leipzig, 1931.

III. CRITICAL AND REFERENCE WORKS

Abrams, M. H., ed. *A Glossary of Literary Terms*. New York, n.d. [1957].
Beißner, Friedrich, Emil Staiger, Friedrich Sengle, Hans Werner Seiffert. *Wieland*. Vier Biberacher Vorträge 1953. Wiesbaden, 1954.
BLACKALL, ERIC A. *The Emergence of German as a Literary Language 1700-1775*. Cambridge, 1959.
Boesch, Bruno, ed., *Deutsche Literaturgeschichte in Grundzügen*. Bern, 1946·
BÖTTIGER, KARL WILHELM. *Christoph Martin Wieland nach seiner Freunde und seinen eigenen Äußerungen*. Leipzig, 1839.
BUDDE, FRITZ. *Wieland und Bodmer*. Berlin, 1910.
CANNAN, GILBERT. *Satire*. New York, n.d.
CANTARINO, BÄRBEL B. "Aloys Blumauer and the Literature of Austrian Englightenment." Diss. University of North Carolina, 1967.
CASSIRER, ERNST. *Die Philosophie der Aufklärung*. Tübingen, 1932.
CRAIG, CHARLOTTE MARIE. "From Folk Legend to Travesty: An Example of Christoph Martin Wieland's Artistic Adaptations," *The German Quarterly*, XLI (May 1968), 369-376.
— "Themes and Style in Christoph Martin Wieland's Fairy Tales: A Comparison with his Sources." Diss. Rutgers, 1964.
Crüger, Johannes, ed., *Johann Christoph Gottsched und die Schweizer J. J. Bodmer und J. J. Breitinger*. Berlin, Stuttgart, 1884.
DE BOOR, HELMUT AND RICHARD NEWALD. *Geschichte der deutschen Literatur von den Anfängen bis zur Gegenwart*. Vols. II, III, 1., V, VI, 1. München, 1961-1963.
EBELING, FRIEDRICH W. *Geschichte der komischen Literatur in Deutschland während der 2. Hälfte des 18. Jahrhunderts*. Vol. III, Leipzig, 1869.
ECONOMOU, GEORGE D'. "Januarie's Sin against Nature: The *Merchant's Tale* And the *Roman de la Rose*," *Comparative Literature*, XVII (1965), 251-257.
ELLIOTT, ROBERT C. *The Power of Satire*. Princeton, 1960.
ERMATINGER, EMIL. *Deutsche Dichtung 1750-1900*. Frankfurt am Main, Bonn, 1961.
— *Die Weltanschauung des jungen Wieland*. Frauenfeld, 1907.
FITZELL, JOHN. *The Hermit in German Literature (From Lessing to Eichendorff)*. (*Studies in The Germanic Languages and Literatures*). Chapel Hill, n.d. [1961].
FLÖGEL, KARL FRIEDRICH. *Geschichte des Grotesk-Komischen*. Leipzig 1862.

FRIEDERICH, WERNER P. *Dante's Fame Abroad. 1350-1850.* Chapel Hill, 1950.
FUCHS, ALBERT. *Les Apports français dans l'oeuvre de Wieland de 1772 à 1789.* Paris, 1934.
GOEDEKE, KARL. *Grundriß zur Geschichte der deutschen Dichtung aus den Quellen.* Vol. IV. Berlin, 1960.
GRIMM, JACOB AND WILHELM. *Deutsches Wörterbuch,* ed. M. Lexer. Vol. XI. Leipzig, 1890.
Der große Brockhaus, "Travestie." Vol. XI of 23 vols. Wiesbaden, 1957.
HARN, EDITH M. *Wieland's Neuer Amadis.* Baltimore, 1928.
HEMPEL, WIDO. "Parodie, Travestie und Pastische. Zur Geschichte von Wort und Sache," *Germanisch-Romanische Monatsschrift,* XV (April 1965), 150-176.
HIGHET, GILBERT. *The Anatomy of Satire.* Princeton, 1962.
HIRZEL, LUDWIG. *Wielands Beziehungen zu den deutschen Romantikern.* Bern, 1904.
JOLLES, ANDRÉ. *Einfache Formen: Legende, Sage, Mythe, Rätsel Spiel, Kasus, Memorabile, Märchen, Witz.* Halle/Saale, 1956.
KAUSCH, K. H. "Die Kunst der Grazie. Ein Beitrag zum Verständnis Wielands," *Jahrbuch der deutschen Schillergesellschaft,* II (1958), 12-42.
KAYSER, WOLFGANG. *Kleines literarisches Lexikon.* Vol. I. Bern, München, 1961.
— *Das sprachliche Kunstwerk.* Bern, München, 1961.
KLEE, GOTTHOLD. "Wielands Gedicht 'Sixt und Klärchen,' sein ursprünglicher Plan und seine Quelle," *Zeitschrift für den deutschen Unterricht,* XIII, xi (1899), 728-730.
KLEIN, JOHANNES. *Geschichte der deutschen Novelle von Goethe bis zur Gegenwart.* 4th ed. Wiesbaden, 1960.
KOCH, MAX. *Das Quellenverhältniß von Wielands Oberon.* Marburg, 1880.
Kohlschmidt, Werner and Wolfgang Mohr, eds. *Reallexikon der deutschen Literaturgeschichte.* 2. Auflage. Vol. III, 1. Lieferung. Berlin, 1966.
KORFF, H. A. *Geist der Goethezeit.* 4 vols. Leipzig, 1923-1953.
KÖRNER, JOSEF. *Bibliographisches Handbuch des deutschen Schrifttums.* Bern, 1949.
KOSCH, WILHELM. *Deutsches Literatur-Lexikon.* Vols. II, IV. Bern, 1953, 1958.
LEUCA, G. "Wieland and the Introduction of Shakespeare into Germany," *The German Quarterly,* XXVIII (1955), 247-255.
MEESSEN, H. J. "Wieland's 'Briefe an einen jungen Dichter,'" *Monatshefte,* XLVII (April-May 1955), 193-208.
MEIER, GEORG FRIEDRICH. *Thoughts on Jesting,* ed. Joseph Jones. Austin, 1947.
MICHEL, VICTOR. *C. M. Wieland, La Formation et l'évolution de son esprit jusqu'en 1772.* Paris, n.d. [1938].

Murray, James A. H. et al., eds., *The Oxford English Dictionary*. Vol. XI of 12 vols. Oxford, 1933, reprinted 1961.
PANZER, FRIEDRICH. *Studien zur germanischen Sagengeschichte*. Vol. II. München, 1912.
PASCAL, ROY. *The German Sturm und Drang*. New York, 1953.
PETSCH, ROBERT. *Deutsche Literaturwissenschaft. Aufsätze zur Begründung der Methode*. Germanische Studien, Heft 222. Berlin, 1940.
— *Wesen und Formen der Erzählkunst*. Halle/Saale, 1934.
PREISENDANZ, WOLFGANG. "Wieland und die Verserzählung des 18. Jahrhunderts," *Germanisch-Romanische Monatsschrift*, XII (January 1962), 17-31.
REED, EUGENE E. "Leibniz, Wieland, and the Combinatory Principle," *The Modern Language Review*, LVI (October 1961), 529-537.
RITTER, ERWIN FRANK. "Johann Baptist von Alxinger. A Literary Profile of the Austrian Enlightenment." Diss. University of North Carolina, 1967.
RÖHRICH, LUTZ. *Märchen und Wirklichkeit*. Wiesbaden, 1956.
SCHLEGEL, AUGUST WILHELM. *Geschichte der deutschen Sprache und Poesie* (Vorlesungen, gehalten an der Universität Bonn seit dem Wintersemester 1818/19). Berlin, 1913.
— *Vorlesungen über dramatische Kunst und Litteratur*, ed. Eduard Böcking. Vol. I. Leipzig, 1846.
— and Friedrich Schlegel, eds., *Athenaeum*. Berlin: 1798-1800. Reprint, Stuttgart, 1960.
SCHNEIDER, FERDINAND JOSEF. *Die deutsche Dichtung der Aufklärungszeit*. Stuttgart, 1948.
— *Die deutsche Dichtung der Geniezeit*. Stuttgart, 1952.
— *Die deutsche Dichtung vom Ausgang des Barocks bis zum Beginn des Klassizismus 1700-1785*. Stuttgart, 1924.
SCHÖNAICH, CHRISTOPH OTTO, FREIHERR VON. *Die ganze Aesthetik in einer Nußschale, oder Neologisches Wörterbuch*, ed. Albert Köster. Leipzig, 1898-1900.
SEIDLER, HERBERT. *Die Dichtung*. Stuttgart, 1959.
SENGLE, FRIEDRICH. *Arbeiten zur deutschen Literatur 1750-1850*. Stuttgart, 1965.
— *Wieland*. Stuttgart, 1949.
SEUFFERT. BERNHARD. *Der Dichter des Oberon*. Sammlung Gemeinnütziger Vorträge, ed. Deutscher Verein zur Verbreitung gemeinnütziger Kenntnis in Prag, Nr. 264. Prag, 1900.
Der Sprachbrockhaus. Wiesbaden, 1959.
STAIGER, EMIL. *Die Kunst der Interpretation*. Zürich, 1961.
STAMM, ISRAEL S. "Wieland and Sceptical Rationalism." *The Germanic Review*, XXXIII (February 1958), 15-29.
STERN, GUY. "Saint or Hypocrite? A study of Wieland's 'Jacinte Episode,'" *The Germanic Review* (April 1954), 96-101.

WASSERZIEHER, ERNST. *Woher? Ableitendes Wörterbuch der deutschen Sprache.* Bonn, 1959.
WELLEK, RENÉ AND AUSTIN WARREN. *Theory of Literature.* New York, 1956.
WILPERT, GERO VON. *Sachwörterbuch der Literatur.* Stuttgart, 1959.
WOLFFHEIM, HANS. *Wielands Begriff der Humanität.* Hamburg, 1949.
WORCESTER, DAVID. *The Art of Satire.* Cambridge, Mass., 1949.

AUTHOR AND TITLE INDEX

Addison, Joseph
The Spectator, 64

Abrams, M. H., ed.
A Glossary of Literary Terms, 5

Alxinger, Johann Baptist von, 17

Anna Amalia, Duchess, 22-23, 92, 112

Anstey, Christopher
The New Bath Guide, 40

Arabian Nights, see Galland

Argens, Jean Baptiste de Boyer, d', 33

Ariosto, Ludovico, 38, 66, 69

Bar, Baron Georg Ludwig von
Epîtres diverses sur des Sujets différents, 34

Baumer, J. W., 36

Bayle, Pierre, 33

Bebel, Heinrich, 13

Beißner, Friedrich, 2-3

Berkhan, F., 17

Bibliothèque Universelle des Romans, 42, 45, 47, 80, 98, 102
Forty Viziers, 98
Gyron-le-Courtois, 42
La Mule sans Frein, 80, 117

Romans de Chevalerie, 42
(see also Tressan)

Blackall, Eric A.
The Emergence of German as a Literary Language 1700-1775, 25

Blumauer, Aloys, 18, 122
Aeneis, 17, 122

Boccaccio, Giovanni, 7
The Decameron, 61

Bodmer, Johann Jakob, 16, 17, 23, 34, 35, 65, 66
Polytimet, 16

Bouhour, Dominique, 125

Brant, Sebastian, 14
Das Narrenschiff, 13

Breitinger, Johann Jakob, 16
Critische Dichtkunst, 33

Brockes, Barthold Heinrich, 33

Bürger, Gottfried August, 16, 17, 18

Le Cabinet des Fées, 88, 105

Cassirer, Ernst
Die Philosophie der Aufklärung, 125, 126

Catullus, Gaius Valerius, 15

Cervantes Saavedra, Miguel de, 51

*The Ingenious Gentleman
Don Quixote de la Mancha*, 36,
51

Chaucer, Geoffrey, 56, 57
The Canterbury Tales, 46, 57
The Merchant's Tale, 46, 57,
59, 60, 61

Chrétien de Troyes, 80

Claudius, Matthias, ed.
Wandsbeck, 16

Cronegk, J. F. von, 16

Dedekind, Friedrich
Grobianus, 14, 70

Democritus, 33

Dryden, John, 15

Ebeling, Friedrich W.
Geschichte der komischen Literatur in Deutschland während der 2. Hälfte des 18. Jahrhunderts, 6

Epistolae virorum obscurorum, 12

Erasmus, Desiderius
Laus stultitiae, 13

Fielding, Henry, 25

Fischart, Johann, 14
Affenteurliche vnd Ungeheurliche Geschichtschrift Vom Leben, rhaten vnd Thaten der for langen weilen Vollen wol beschraiten Helden vnd Herrn Grandgusier, Gargantoa vnd Pantagruel, Königen von Vtopien vnd Ninenreich, 15
(see also *Geschichtklitterung*)
Aller Praktik Großmutter, 14
Die Flöhhaz, 14
Geschichtklitterung, 14, 15
Das Jesuiterhütlein, 15
Podagrammatisch Trostbüchlein, 13
Die Wunderlichst Vnerhörtest Legend vnd Beschreibung Des Angeführten, Quartirten, Gevierten vnd Viereckechten Vierhörnigen Hütleins, 15 (see also *Das Jesuiterhütlein*)

Fontenelle, Bernard Le Bovier de, 33

Frischlin, Nicodemus, 13

Fuchs, Albert
Les Apports français dans l'oeuvre de Wieland de 1772 à 1789, 20

Galland, Antoine, 88, 92, 93, 94, 96
Arabian Nights, 88, 91, 92, 101
Story of the Fisherman, 101
The Story of the Grecian King and the Physician Douban, 101
The Story of the Three Calendars, Sons of Kings; and of the Five Ladies of Bagdad, 92

Gellert, Christian Fürchtegott, 34

Gerstenberg, Heinrich Wilhelm von, 16
Schleswig letters, 16
Ugolino, 16

Geßner, Salomon, 38, 67, 71, 72

Gleim, Johann Wilhelm von, 17, 34, 40

Goethe, Johann Wolfgang von, 18, 23, 30, 46, 102
Anektode [sic] zu den Freuden des jungen Werther, 18
Götter, Helden und Wieland, 18
Unterhaltungen deutscher Ausgewanderten, 61

Gottfried von Straßburg, 13

Göttinger Musen-Almanach, 16

Gottsched, Johann Christoph, 16, 34, 65
Der sterbende Cato, 16

Grimm, Jacob and Wilhelm, 88
Deutsches Wörterbuch, 4
Der große Brockhaus, 7
Gruber, J. G., ed.
C. M. Wielands sämmtliche Werke, 23, 38, 63, 69, 73, 74, 80, 84, 117, 118
Gryphius, Andreas
Absurda Comica oder Herr Peter Squentz, 15
Horribilicribrifax, 15
Gyron-le-Courtois, 42 (see also Wieland, *Geron der Adeliche*)
Hagedorn, Friedrich von, 17, 33
Haller, Albrecht von, 16, 33
Hamilton, Anthony, 72
Bélier, 38
Les Quatre Facardins, 38
Helvetius, Claude Adrien, 66
Hempel, Wido
"Parodie, Travestie und Pastische. Zur Geschichte von Wort und Sache," 6-7
Herder, Johann Gottfried, 23, 84, 105
Highet, Gilbert
The Anatomy of Satire, 11
Hofmannswaldau, Christian Hofmann von, 15
Hölty, Ludwig, 17
Homer, 34
Horace (Horatius Flaccus, Quintus), 15, 17, 19, 64
Huon de Bordeaux, 46
Kayser, Wolfgang, ed.
Kleines literarisches Lexikon, 4
Klee, Gotthold, 109, 116
"Wielands Gedicht 'Sixt und Klärchen,' sein ursprünglicher Plan und seine Quelle," 109, 116
Kleist, Ewald von, 17
Klopstock, Friedrich Gottlieb, 16, 34
Koch, Max
Das Quellenverhältniß von Wielands Oberon, 49, 51, 57, 61
La Fontaine, Jean de
Contes et Nouvelles, 63, 69, 70
La Coupe Enchantée, see *Contes et Nouvelles*
Lange, Samuel Gotthold, 34
La Roche, Michael, 71
La Roche, Sophie, 37, 66
Legrand d'Aussy, Pierre Jean Baptiste, 84, 117
Contes Dévots pour servir de Suite aux Fabliaux et Contes du treizième Siècle, 84
Du Prévot d'Aquilée, 84
Fabliaux ou Contes du douzième et du treizième Siècle, 80, 117
Lays de l'Oiselet, 117
La Mule sans Frein, 80, 117; see also *Bibliothèque Universelle des Romans*
Leibniz, Gottfried Wilhelm, 33
Lessing, Gotthold Ephraim, 16
8. Literaturbrief, 21
13. Literaturbrief, 21
Philotas, 16
Lichtenberg, Georg Christoph, 18
Limberg, Johannes, 109, 110, 111, 114
Das im Jahr 1708. lebende und schwebende Eisenach, 109
Denkwürdige Reisebeschreibungen durch Deutschland, Italien,

Spanien, Portugal, England, und Schweiz, 109
Der Mittelstein, 110 (see *Das im Jahr 1708. lebende und schwebende Eisenach*)

Lohenstein, Daniel Kasper von, 15

Lolli, Giovanni Battista, 15

Lucianus Samosatensis, 3, 35, 36, 37, 66, 67, 68
Sämtliche Werke, trans. C. M. Wieland, 73, 74, 75, 76, 77, 78, 80

Lucretius, Carus Titus, 33
De rerum natura, 34

Lukian, see Lucianus Samosatensis

Machiavelli, Niccolò, 7

Marmontel, Jean François
Contes moreaux, 63

Martini, Fritz and Hans Werner Seiffert, eds.,
Christoph Martin Wieland, Werke, 1

Michaelis, J. B.
Leben und Taten des teuren Helden Aeneas, 17

Milton, John, 34
Paradise Lost, 64, 65

Minnedichtung, 13

Montaigne, Michel Eyquem, 7

Montalvo, García Ordóñez de
Amadis de Gaula, 40

Moreau, Jacques, 15

Murner, Thomas, 14
Die Gäuchmatt, 14
Die Narrenbeschwörung, 14
Die Schelmenzunft, 14

Musäus, Johann Karl, 88
Der deutsche Grandison. Auch eine Familiengeschichte, 18
Grandison II oder die Geschichte des Herrn von N. in Briefen entworfen, 18
Volksmärchen der Deutschen, 88

Neidhart von Reuenthal, 13

Newald, Richard, 53

Das Nibelungenlied, 13

Nicolai, Friedrich, 18
Die Freuden des jungen Werthers, 18, 70
Vertraute Briefe von Adelheid B* an ihre Freundin Julie S*, 18

Ovidius Naso, Publius, 17
Metamorphoses, VII, 69
The Story of Cephalus and Procris, 69

"The Passion of Doctor Martin Luther," 14

Petsch, Robert
Wesen und Formen der Erzählung, 6

Pope, Alexander, 40, 56
Dunciad, 65
January and May, 57, 59, 60, 61
The Rape of the Lock, 40

Prior, Matthew, 72
Alma, or the Progress of the Mind, 72

Rabelais, François
Gargantua et Pantagruel, 15
Pantagrueline Prognosticatio, 14

Reallexikon der deutschen Literaturgeschichte, 4, 12, 15, 16

Reinmar, 13

Richardson, Samuel, 18

Riedel, Friedrich Just, 71, 73

143

Rollenhagen, Georg
Der Froschmeuseler, 14

Romans de Chevalerie, 42 (see also *Bibliothèque Universelle des Romans*)

Rost, Johann, Christoph
Schäfererzählungen, 63

Rowe, Nicholas, 34

Scarron, Paul, 15
Roman Comique, 42
La Dame Invisible, 42
Virgile travesty, 4
Le Virgile travesti ,en vers burlesques, 17

Scheidt, Kaspar, 14

Schiller, Friedrich von, 17

Schlegel, Friedrich, 18

Schlegel, Johann Elias
Canut, 16

Schneider, Ferdinand Josef
Die deutsche Dichtung der Aufklärungszeit, 3, 23, 26
Die deutsche Dichtung vom Ausgang des Barocks bis zum Beginn des Klassizismus 1700-1785, 88

Schönaich, Christoph Otto, Freiherr von, 16
Die ganze Aesthetik in einer Nußschale, oder Neologisches Wörterbuch, 65

Schwabe, Johann Jakob, 16

Schwankliteratur, 13

Seiffert, Hans Werner (see Martini, Beißner)

Sengle, Friedrich
"Von Wielands Epenfragmenten zum 'Oberon,'" *Arbeiten zur deutschen Literatur 1750-1850*, 29, 39, 56
Wieland, 1, 23, 35, 42, 45, 60, 66, 69, 71, 74, 80, 95, 100, 101, 105, 107, 112, 113, 118, (see also Beißner)

Shakespeare, William, 21, 37, 56, 59
A Midsummer-Night's Dream, 46, 59

Der Sprach-Brockhaus, 7

Staël-Holstein, Anne Louise Germaine de, 23,
De l'Allemagne, 47

Staiger, Emil
(see Beißner)

Stamm, I. S.
"Wieland and Sceptical Rationalism," 21

Sterne, Lawrence, 25, 39

Stoppe, Daniel
Neue Fabeln oder moralische Gedichte, 16

Swift, Jonathan, 35, 66

Tasso, Bernardo
Amadigi, 40

Thomson, James, 34
The Seasons, 63

Tieck, Ludwig
Prinz Zerbino, 18

Tressan, Louis de la Vergne
Huon de Bordeaux, 46ff.

Triller, Daniel Wilhelm, 16

Vergilius Maro, Publius, 15, 17, 34
Aeneid, 15

Verulamius, 110

Voltaire, François, 22, 33, 35

Voß, Johann Heinrich, 16, 17

Walther von der Vogelweide, 13

Wasserzieher, Ernst
Woher? Ableitendes Wörterbuch der deutschen Sprache, 7

Weckherlin, Georg Rudolf, 68
Weise, Christian
  Lustspiel von einer zweifachen Poetenzunft, 15
Weisse, Christian F., 73
Wellek, René and Austin Warren
  Theory of Literature, 121
Wernher der Gartenaere
  Meier Helmbrecht, 13
Wernicke, Christian, 15
Wieland, Christoph Martin, 1, et passim
  Die Abenteuer des Don Sylvio von Rosalva, 24, 28, 35ff., 39, 71
  Alceste, 17, 18
  Ankündigung einer Dunciade für die Deutschen, 65
  Anti-Ovid, oder die Kunst zu lieben, 34
  Aspasia, 74 (see also *Griechische Erzählungen*)
  Aurora und Cefalus, 67, 69f. (see also *Komische Erzählungen*)
  Ausgewählte Briefe an verschiedene Freunde in den Jahren 1751. bis 1810. geschrieben, und nach der Zeitfolge geordnet, II (*AB*), 40, 72, 84
  Ausgewählte Werke, ed. Friedrich Beißner, 1
  Auswahl denkwürdiger Briefe, ed. Ludwig Wieland (*DB*), 24, 25, 38, 67, 71, 72, 73, 122
  Balsora, 64 (see also *Moralische Erzählungen*) *Clementina von Porretta*, 35
  Diana und Endymion, 67 (see also *Komische Erzählungen*)
  Dschinnistan oder auserlesene Feen- und Geistermärchen, 27-28, 91, 105ff., 117
  Erzählungen, 34 (see also *Moralische Erzählungen*), 63-65
  Gandalin oder Liebe um Liebe, 42ff.
  Geron der Adeliche, 42
  Geschichte der Abderiten, 41-42
  Geschichte des Agathon, 23, 71
  "Geschichte der drei Kalender," 92 (see *Geschichte des weisen Danischmend und der drei Kalender*)
  Die Geschichte des Prinzen Biribinker, 36 (see *Die Abenteuer des Don Sylvio von Rosalva*)
  Geschichte des weisen Danischmend und der drei Kalender, 41, 51, 92f.
  Der goldne Spiegel oder die Könige von Scheschian, 41, 91
  Griechische Erzählungen, 74
  Hann und Gulpenhee oder zu viel gesagt ist nichts gesagt, 98ff.
  Hermann, 34
  Das Hexameron von Rosenhain, 61
  Idris und Zenide, 29, 37ff.
  Juno und Ganymed, 69 (see also *Komische Erzählungen*)
  Klelia und Sinibald, 84
  Kombabus, 26, 73ff. (see also *Griechische Erzählungen*)
  Komische Erzählungen, 37, 67ff., 74 (see also *Griechische Erzählungen*)
  Lady Johanna Gray, 35
  Lobgesang auf die Liebe, 34
  Der Mönch und die Nonne auf dem Mittelstein, 107ff. (see also *Sixt und Clärchen*)
  Moralische Erzählungen, 63-65
  Musarion, 23, 72, 73
  Die Natur der Dinge, 34
  Der neue Amadis, 37, 40f.

Oberon, 17, 26, 42, 43, 45ff., 74
Pervonte oder die Wünsche, 102ff., 112
Die Salamandrin und die Bildsäule, 106f. (see also *Dschinnistan*)
Sämmtliche Werke, ed. J. G. Gruber, 2, *et passim* (see also Gruber)
Schach Lolo, oder das göttliche Recht der Gewalthaber, 26, 51, 52, 101f.
Seraphina, 112
Shakespeare Translations, 21, 37, 71
Der Sieg der Natur über die Schwärmerei, 35 (see also *Die Abenteuer des Don Sylvio von Rosalva*)
Sixt und Clärchen, 28-29, 52, 64, 84, 107ff., (see also *Der Mönch und die Nonne auf dem Mittelstein*)
Das Sommermährchen, 80ff., 117, 118
Der Stein der Weisen, 106 (see also *Dschinnistan*)
Der Teutsche Merkur, 27, 108, 112ff.,
Über die vorgebliche Abnahme des menschlichen Geschlechts, 91
Über den Hang der Menschen an Magie und Geistererscheinungen zu glauben, 28, 89
Das Urtheil des Paris, 67
(see also *Komische Erzählungen*)
Der Vogelsang oder die drei Lehren, 29, 112, 117ff.
Von den Pygmäen, 33
Von der syrischen Göttin, 73
Die Wasserkufe, 52, 64, 84ff., 118
Werke, XXX, 27-28, 89
Werke, eds. Fritz Martini and Hans Werner Seiffert, 1
Das Wintermährchen, 51, 93ff., 112
"Der Fischer und der Geist," 93ff.
"Der König der schwarzen Inseln," 93, 96f.
Zemin und Gulindy, 64 (see also *Moralische Erzählungen*)
Zwölf moralische Briefe in Versen, 34

Wilpert, Gero von
Sachwörterbuch der Literatur, 5-6
Wittenweiler, Heinrich
Der Ring, 13
Wolff, Christian, 33
Wolfram von Eschenbach
Tristan und Isolde, 13
Worcester, David
The Art of Satire, 11
Young, Edward, 34
Zimmermann, Johann Georg, 72

www.ingramcontent.com/pod-product-compliance
Lightning Source LLC
Chambersburg PA
CBHW031315150426
43191CB00005B/240